A Guide to Organising Your Family History Records

No. 4 in the Jewish Ancestor Series

Written by
Rosemary Wenzerul

Chairman, JGSGB Education Committee
Member of Council

זכר ימות עולם בינו שנות דר-ודר
שאל אביך ויגדך זקניך ויאמרו-לך :
Remember the days of old, consider the years of many generations:
Ask thy father, and he will declare unto thee: Thine elders, and they will tell thee.
Deuteronomy XXX11 v.7   דברים לב ז

103637084

Published by
The Jewish Genealogical Society of Great Britain
Registered Charity No. 1022738
PO Box 13288, London, N3 3WD.
E-mail: publications@jgsgb.org.uk
Web site: www.jgsgb.org.uk

First edition January 2004

Copyright © Rosemary Wenzerul

ISBN 0 9537669 4 2

Front cover designed by
Rosemary Hoffman and Derek Wenzerul

Printed and bound in the United Kingdom
by the Alden Group, Oxford
☎ 01865 253200

CONTENTS

ILLUSTRATIONS

INTRODUCTION

A Guide to Organising Your Family History Records is the fourth publication in the '*Jewish Ancestor*' series. It is written in the simplest way, to help Family Historians who have just started their family history and those who have gathered a lot of information about their family and need help with putting it in order. Whether you have a computer or not this book provides examples, advice and suggestions on how to keep your records in order by the most up-to-date methods plus ideas to enlarge the social history of your family. There are a couple of technical sections which, unfortunately, could not be avoided. The section on preservation is intended to help keep your documents and photographs in the best possible condition so as to enable them to be enjoyed by future generations. Please refer to the Glossary for unfamiliar terms.

When thinking about a suitable filing system, it is important to introduce one which is simple, yet efficient, so that future generations will be able to pick up where you left off.

How many of us have visited relatives and in the course of conversation made notes on any scrap of paper to hand with the intention of adding the information to our family history records on our return home. If this is not done immediately, the information may be mislaid or the fuller details forgotten?

Keeping records in order is extremely important and the chapter headed 'Document Links' illustrates the relationships between sets of documents. It is only a guide and is intended for the reader to decide which documents to include.

I am indebted to **Petra Laidlaw** and **Else Churchill**, for their constructive and in-depth guidance and advice which was greatly appreciated. I would also like to thank **Peter Glass** for proof reading, **Rosemary Hoffman** for her section on the census and **Judith Samson** for taking so much trouble in checking the sections. **Henry and Dianah Ellis, Cyril Fox, June Jones and Jeanette Rosenberg** who have also contributed to this publication. In addition, I would like to thank **Derek Wenzerul** for his continual assistance with the technical side of producing the guides.

Rosemary Wenzerul   *January 2004*

THE JEWISH GENEALOGICAL SOCIETY OF GREAT BRITAIN

The Jewish Genealogical Society of Great Britain (JGSGB) is the premier society for Jewish genealogy in Great Britain. The Society encourages genealogical research and promotes the preservation of Jewish genealogy records and resources, sharing information amongst members.

Beginners and experienced researchers help one another to learn and discover more about Jewish genealogy. Members have the opportunity to meet like-minded people at central and regional meetings, group meetings and informal meetings in members' homes.

The Society offers its members:

Beginners: Family History Workshops, research guidance, publications and computer courses.

Experienced Genealogists: Extensive library and archive, annual seminar, special interest groups, research visits, genealogical workshops.

For everyone: Regular newsletter, quarterly Journal '*Shemot*', On-line discussion group, Monthly meetings, Regional groups, Members only website, JGSGB Family Finder, Informal meetings at home.

Web site: www.jgsgb.org.uk
Our web site has a resource-packed section reserved for JGSGB members only and links to almost every conceivable genealogical web site.

Membership Application Form is on page 116 or on the JGSGB web site.

WHY IT IS IMPORTANT
TO BE ORGANISED

There are many reasons why it is important to be organised about the documents and data that you have collected:

- First of all, if you don't have a filing system in place, you will never be able to locate your data or bring your family history together.

- Secondly, depending on the amount of data you have collected, it is important to look at the various ways of preserving the material.

- Thirdly, a system needs to be designed to allow easy retrieval of documents, both for yourself and for future generations.

To do this you will need to know the various options available to you. For example:

- Filing arrangements

- Preservation methods

- Uses of new technology

Having looked at the above options you will then need to decide the way in which you wish to approach this. For example filing by:

- Surname

- Individual

- Date

- Theme

What do you wish to achieve from collecting the above data:

- Family narrative in book form

- CD

- Form a specific collection

- Family History Project

All these points need to be clarified to enable you to get the most out of your family history.

The following pages will cover all aspects of how to do this.

WHERE SHOULD I START?

WORK IN PROGRESS

Before collecting any data, it is a good idea to purchase an expanding file for your work in progress and a couple of large A4 ring-binder folders with dividers for filing.

EXPANDING FILES

Expanding files are best used as intermediate files for work-in-progress prior to analysis and final filing, not as permanent stores. They will keep your documents in alphabetical order and they are easy to use. In addition, they hold a substantial amount. They would be helpful to keep your papers in until you file them into your main folders. It may be easier to change the alphabetical index into the headings you wish to use for your documents, for example certificates, correspondence, newspapers, photographs, wills etc.

These files are sometimes known as 'concertina' or 'accordion' files.

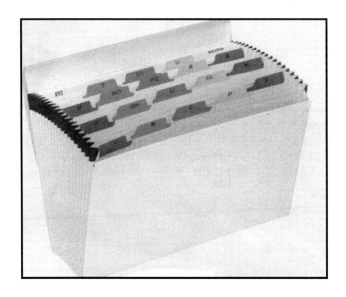

RING-BINDER FOLDERS

Use each section of your ring-binder folder for a different part of the family. This will enable you to transfer the information from one folder to another as your family history expands. Ring-binder folders come in a variety of colours. You may wish to buy all the same colour or different colours for each section of your family history. If you have a very large family, break your documentation down into manageable sections.

For instance, if your grandparents had eight children, it would be absolutely impossible to file all the information you have collected into one file. Therefore, keep a folder for your grandparents and start other folders for the children and their families. By using dividers to separate each family, it will be easier to locate them.

LABELLING YOUR FOLDERS

The examples on pages 14 and 15, illustrate how to label your ring-binder folders. By numbering the folders, you will be able to keep them in the order they should be referred to.

By adding the letters a,b,c etc. after each number, this will give more scope should you run out of space in one or more of the folders.

The ring-binder folders will line up next to one another on your shelf as the example on page 13 shows. If you purchase your folders with the 'metal ring in the spine', it will help when pulling them out from a shelf or cupboard. Some folders have small metal edges which will prevent the corners being damaged. They are slightly more expensive, but worth the extra money.

PASSING YOUR COLLECTION TO A LIBRARY OR ARCHIVE

Should you accumulate a very large collection of important documents, photographs and artefacts then perhaps it would be sensible to contact a specific museum or archive to see whether they would be interested in holding it on your behalf.

If this were the case, then it would not be satisfactory to use ring-binder folders. The archivist would immediately remove material from ring-binders as it is vulnerable to theft or damage from the holes punched into the documents. This applies even if you use plastic wallets. Those found in most stationers, are generally not considered to be archivally suitable.

Archives and libraries would prefer to bind typescripts and therefore adequate margins should be left for this to be done.

STORAGE

If you find you have storage problems at home, there are single or stacking file storage systems available on the market which will accommodate your ring-binder folders. Alternatively, there are storage boxes with flip-top lids.

Some storage boxes have dividers within the framework so that each ring-binder folder fits into a specific slot. The only problem with these is that you can only fill your folder up to a certain point; otherwise it will not fit into the space provided. Therefore, something similar to the illustration on the previous page might be a better option.

DIVIDERS

Should you decide to use plastic folders within the ring-binder, ensure when you purchase the dividers, that you buy the A4 extra wide ones, otherwise the plastic folders will stick out beyond the dividers and the names on the edges will not be visible. Obviously, if you are just going to file your papers direct into the ring-binder, then the regular sized ones will suffice.

Dividers are usually sold in packs 10. Look carefully at these before buying them as some manufacturers only produce small areas on which to write, whereas others have quite long areas. You may find that 'buff' coloured dividers are cheaper than coloured. It is well worth checking. Some stationery catalogues are cheaper than shops and will deliver the following day.

LABELS

FAMILY TREE PART 1a	FAMILY TREE PART 1b	FAMILY TREE PART 2
GOLDSTON	**GOLDSTON**	
Isaac and Rose		Family Memories Family Recipes Freemasonry
Agnes Alfred Frances Joseph	Leonard Marjory Nehemiah Sim	Medical Conditions Memorabilia Newspapers Publications

FAMILY TREE PART 3	FAMILY TREE PART 4	FAMILY TREE PART 5
WAR	**VITAL RECORDS**	**RELATED FAMILIES**
1914-1918	Birth	Barnett
1939-1945	Death	Benjamin
	Ketubot	Feldman
	Marriage	Molen/Vandermolen
	Probate/Wills	Wenzerul

FAMILY TREE PART 7a	FAMILY TREE PART 8 PROPERTY	FAMILY TREE PART 9 MISC
LETTERS	Addresses	Address Indexes
	Map locations	b,m,d Indexes
A - J	Old O/S Maps	Grave Index
	Public Houses	Naming Patterns
	Synagogues	Negative Index

Labels should all be produced in alphabetical order as shown above. However, this is entirely up to each individual. You may prefer to put the names of the children as shown in Family Tree Part 1a and 1b in age order with the eldest child shown first.

Under the heading 'miscellaneous' include small sections of your family history which wouldn't require a whole ring-binder e.g. negative film index or naming patterns. Don't forget, that the headings used on the outside of your folders should be the same as those on your dividers.

DATES

Remember how important dates are and will be to future generations. When writing down dates the full date is preferable e.g. 21 March 1946 rather than 21/03/46. The latter could be mistaken for 1746 or 1846. Careful attention to American dates should be made as they tend to put the month first.

If you so wished, certain documents could be filed in date order for example, correspondence.

REINFORCEMENT RINGS

You may decide not to use plastic folders and file your documents straight into the ring-binder folders. In this case you need to purchase some reinforcement rings, which are made of polypropylene and will help prevent your pages being torn. However, I would not advise putting these onto very fragile original documents as the glue may, in the long term, cause a problem.

METHODS OF PRESERVATION

As you will be taking the trouble of organising all your documents and photographs in an orderly system, the first thing you should do is make sure they are safe from the ravages of time. Old newspaper cuttings often yellow, they can crumble into dust. Photographs can lose their colour and fade. Photocopies and faxes might survive only a few years. You should be aiming to build up a collection that will last for generations, and this takes some planning.

The following should be taken into account:

- a safe location
- avoidance of direct light
- avoidance of excess heat and damp
- avoidance of acidic paper
- avoidance of certain plastic covers
- preservation of photographic images

A SAFE LOCATION

A safe place will have controlled temperature, relative humidity, good air flow and no natural or fluorescent light. An attic will be better than a damp cellar, and a workroom better still. But do not leave it at that. Back-up your data and keep a copy somewhere else entirely, in case of a fire, flood or burglary: these things do happen. If you have a particularly valuable collection of, say, letters, diaries or photographs, consider taking copies for the family and giving the originals to a museum or archive for safekeeping – they will always be able to do a better job of it.

AVOID DIRECT LIGHT

Light unfortunately will cause fading of many documents and photographs. It is important, therefore, that you avoid direct sun or bright light of any kind falling onto your documents or photographs etc. You might have noticed when visiting museums and stately homes that some of the rooms have subdued lighting and are relatively dark and in some cases, heavy curtains are drawn to prevent damage to very valuable paintings and artefacts by direct sunlight.

AVOID EXCESS HEAT AND DAMP

Commonsense prevails here. Be aware of where you intend to store your documents and photographs. Check there isn't a radiator, boiler or hot water pipe beneath your bookcase, or that the place where you intend storing your photographs or papers isn't near to the bathroom. The latter could cause condensation and eventual mould and staining. Direct storage on concrete floors should be avoided e.g. in a garage.

ACIDIC PAPER

Acidic paper is a problem as it is prone to disintegration. Even if paper is free of acid, over a period of time the presence of chemicals or pollutants from your hands or from the atmosphere will lead to the formation of acid.

There are special acid-free papers on the market, used by archives and museums which are expected to last up to 500 years. You might use these to preserve newspaper cuttings or old letters. Just think how quickly newspapers change colour and deteriorate. Photocopying them on ordinary copy paper will do nothing to help preservation, but on acid-free paper will give them a much longer life. Better still, use your word processor to transcribe them, and keep one version on your computer and a second printed out with durable inks on acid-free paper. Try not to fold documents as in time the documents may disintegrate where the fold has been.

PLASTIC COVERS

Ensure you purchase Acid-Free plastic covers which will not lift the print from your documents. These should be made of Polyester not from PVC (or branded as 'Melinex') as the covers deteriorate and become highly acidic and will eventually destroy the documents you are trying to preserve.

However, the Polyester covers cost several times more than the PVC ones.

LAMINATORS
Laminating your documents will NOT help preserve them. If the document is very fragile the heat from the lamination process may damage it further. Once a document or photograph is laminated it can never be removed. In addition, documents can still deteriorate within the lamination.

PHOTOGRAPHIC MATERIAL
It is absolutely essential to preserve photographic images. The same rules apply as above – if you do not keep photographs in the correct conditions they will fade, or the edges will curl up. They must be kept out of direct sunlight, heat and damp and stored flat.

Colour photographs and Polaroid prints are a problem to preserve as their life expectancy is around 30 years, whereas black and white prints will last in excess of 100 years and negatives even longer. Obviously, you cannot save an image forever but at least it is well worth the effort to try.

As you will have noticed on the television history programmes, most archivists handle photographs and documents with (lintless) cotton gloves. These will act as a barrier between the documents and the acids which are found on your hands. If you are going to store your photographs in an album, ensure that the pages are Polypropylene and that they have Acid-Free paper inserts. Do not use adhesive tapes, staples, pins, metal paper clips, rubber bands or glue. Most glues will, long term, cause a chemical reaction and destroy the photograph. Acid-Free Photo Corners or Acid-Free Double Sided Craft Mounts will be far safer to use. Small tears in paper can be repaired with archival document repair tape. Measure the tear and only use this amount of tape to cover the area. Although using archival document repair tape is quick, a major drawback is that it often does not adhere well. It may be necessary to use a warm iron covered by some blotting paper to ensure the repair tape sticks. Having said this, paper tears repaired with archival tape will never be as strong or last as long as those repaired with methyl cellulose paste.

Traditional Acid Free Photo Corners

Fotoecken
coins photo
fotohoekjes

Acid Free Double Sided Craft Mounts

Fotoekleber
colle-photos
fotosplitjes

Ask your stationer or local photographic shop for advice or if they are unable to help, contact the National Preservation Office who will either answer your question or point you in the right direction (details on page 109). Never try to remove old adhesive tape from documents or photographs – this can be done, but I would suggest that you leave it to the experts.

In addition, most photographic shops or good stationers will have pens which are suitable for writing on the reverse of photographic prints and will not damage your photographs - ideally use an HB pencil.

Avoid using a biro on the reverse of your photographs as these tend to indent into the paper and felt-tip pens will run if the photograph becomes damp. If you use ink (which you should preferably avoid) – ensure it is completely dry in case it marks other photographs.

Always retain the negatives in case the original photographs have become damaged or accidentally destroyed. Negatives should be kept in a cool, dry, dark place. There are folders made especially for negatives which may be purchased at most photographic stores. These come with an index sheet at the front where you can write down details of each negative.

In addition, some film processors will supply a 6"x4" index print card with your prints which will show each print with the number against it. This is very helpful and should be kept with your negatives as it is easier to look at these than hold each set of negatives up to the light to find a specific print.

Ensure photographic albums are supported so they don't collapse at the spine. (Further information on photography see page 63).

USE OF PHOTOCOPIERS
It is good photocopying practice to ensure that you do not exert pressure on the spine of the book. Never open a volume more that 180°. Provide adequate support to pages whilst the item is being placed on the platen. Photographs should never be left on the platen as the heat may cause the surface emulsion to peel and the paper to curl. Some libraries have edge glass platens for book photocopying, where the book folds over the edge and only has to open 90-120°.
(*Photocopying of Library and Archive Material* – National Preservation Office, Preservation Management Series) (See page 110).

COMPUTERS
It is worthwhile keeping copies of everything on your computer, as well as the original documents. Digitising documents and photographs is a good way to preserve them, and gives you a

freely accessible database. Copies can be distributed quickly and cheaply to other members of your family. That way, you keep your handling of the originals down to a minimum, which in itself should give them longer life and you have a digital version that can be preserved almost indefinitely as long as you make sure you transfer it ever time you get a new computer!

There are books available on the subject, so it might be worth your while to visit your local library and ask for their help.

BACK-UP YOUR DATA
Most important of all, remember at the end of every day to back-up all of the data on your computer. This can be done on a floppy disc, zip-disc or writable CD.

Whatever system you decide to use to back-up your system, DON'T leave the disc next to your PC. Keep your back-up in a different room and leave a copy with a friend or relative. If you had a fire, flood or lightning strike, both the computer and the disc would be destroyed and you would have lost all of your work.

Keep magnetic storage media e.g. floppy or zip discs or tapes away from magnetic fields which can corrupt or destroy the data. Do not leave them on top of your screen as the monitor may have strong magnetic fields.

When using floppy discs, ensure you 'lock' the disc by sliding the catch. This will ensure that the disc isn't accidentally overwritten.

NEW TECHNOLOGY
It is important to update the method of archival storage of computer records as the technology changes. For example, data stored on 8" or 5¼" floppy discs or cassette type tapes is inaccessible on current model computers.

COMPUTER VIRUSES

If you use your computer for e-mail or to access the internet, or you receive data in computer readable format, it is essential that you invest in anti-virus and firewall computer software to protect your computer and your valuable data.

There are a number of reputable suppliers of such software, but you must ensure that you have a subscription that permits you to down-load regular updates as new versions of viruses are found daily.

It is suggested that you down-load updates at least once a week.

Virus check any data given to you in a computer readable format (discs etc) before loading it onto your computer. Do not open attachments sent with e-mails unless you know the sender and expect the attachment from them. Even then, ensure that the attachment is scanned before being opened.

As mentioned above, new viruses appear every day and it is just not worth the risk of losing all of your data because you haven't installed some protection.

SUPPLIERS OF ARCHIVAL STORAGE MEDIA

There is an extensive list available from the National Preservation Office, The British Library, 96 Euston Road, London, NW1 2DB. Tel: 020 7412 7612   Fax: 020 7412 7796 E-mail: npo@bl.uk   Web site: www.bl.uk/services/preservation

Acid-Free Photo Corners or Acid-Free Double Sided Craft Mounts are manufactured by Peregrine Stationery, Aerodex Floyd, Tingwick Road Industrial Park, Buckingham, Bucks. MK18 1FY. Tel/Fax: 01280 813095.

Acid-Free Photograph, Slide and CD Plastic Covers are manufactured by the following two manufacturers: Arrowfile, PO Box 88, Southampton, SO14 OZA. Fax: 087 0241 2198. Web site: www.arrowfile.com.

Philip Hand, Papersafe 2 Green Bank, Adderley, Market Drayton, Shropshire TF9 3TH. Tel: 01630 652217 Fax: 0870 054 8747. Web site: www.papersafe.demon.co.uk

---

In this section, there is a lot to take in. You may be inclined to leave it for another day, but you do not need to ask far before you will find someone whose life's work has been ruined by fire, flood, theft or computer virus, or simply inattention to fragile old documents. It could happen to you much more easily than you might think ...... don't let it!

FAMILY NAMES

Sorting out the names of your family may sound a very easy thing to do, but it can become very complicated if you don't start a family tree as soon as possible and arrange the families into some sort of order by generation.

It is very likely that you will find within your family that first names are repeated over and over again. It is generally customary in the Jewish Religion for *Ashkenazim* to name their children after the dead and *Sephardim* after the living. As a result the same combination of given name and surname can be repeated time and again through the generations, and it is important that all these people do not get mixed up. A genealogical software program will enable you to sort them all out into generations.

Agnes Barnett (nee-Nunes-Martines b. 1852	Agnes Goldston b.1.7.1900	Agnes Myers b. 1906	Agnes Benjamin b.6.8.1909	Agnes Molen b.2.5.1910	Agnes Barnett b.10.2.1917
Sim Alfred Goldston b.2.4.1871	Alfred Goldston b.23.6.1898	David Sim Alfred Cohen b.15.9.1922	Alfred Levy b.16.2.1937	John Sim Alfred Davis b. 2.9.1954	
Baron Barnett b.4.5.1848	Cyril Baron Benjamin b.11.5.1906	Peter Baron Barnett b.17.11.1908	Roger Baron Barnett b. 25.2.1917	David Baron Silver b. 2.1.1923	

You may be tempted to draw your tree by hand. If you have all the data you want – and if you have good clear handwriting – this may actually be a better way of doing it than using a computer. (The computer's design instructions are relatively inflexible, and it may take several pages to print something that you could write perfectly clearly on one.) The downside with doing it by hand comes when you need to add, or amend any of the existing entries.

As the example below shows, the handwritten tree can quickly become a mess.

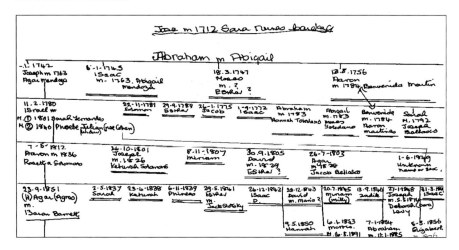

As you will see from the following three examples of family tree charts, there are many ways of drawing a family tree. It depends what you want out of it. The wheel chart is a very commercial way of displaying one person's direct ancestry – but it won't show their brothers or sisters, aunts, uncles or cousins. The box chart is a good way of showing all these lateral links – but you can soon run out of space. The tree chart accommodates the lateral links much more economically in space terms, but it is less easy to read at a glance than the box chart.

Tree Chart

```
great grandfather——┬—great uncle
m. great grandmother │  m. great aunt(marriage)
                     ├—grand father————————┬—father x—————————┬—brother x
                     │  m. grand mother     │  m. mother x     ├—myself x
                     │                      │                  └—sister x
                     │                      │
                     │                      ├—uncle x
                     │                      └—aunt x
                     │
                     └—great aunt—————————————┬—male cousin
                        m. great uncle (marriage) │  m. wife
                                              └—female cousin
                                                 m. husband
```

Box Chart

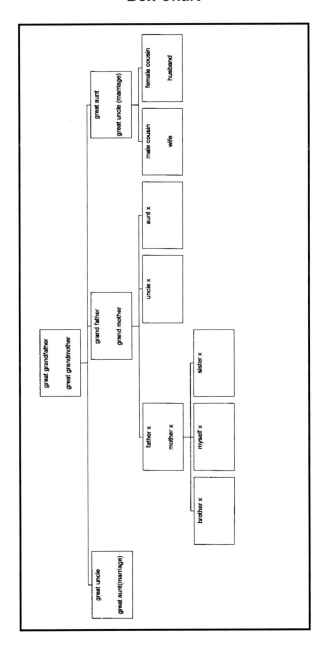

Wheel Chart

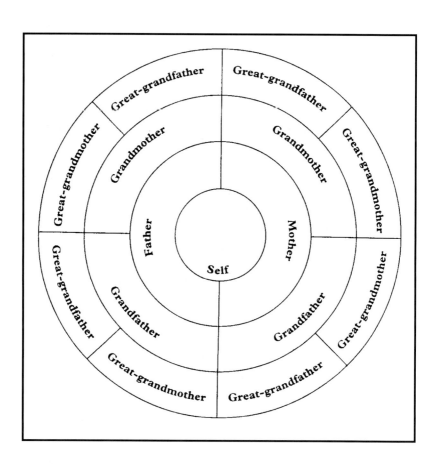

NUMBERING SYSTEMS

There has been a lot of work done on numbering systems especially in the United States.

The easiest way if you are starting from scratch is to make yourself No. 1, your parents 2 and 3 and your grandparents 4 and 5, then continue from there. Having said this, the following example of a descendant tree shows the earliest ancestor as 1, their children as 2, their grandchildren as 3 etc.

If you use a computer program for recording your data, then it will automatically allocate the numbers for you as the following example of a descendant tree indicates:

1 John Gold b: 28 February 1869 12 Artillery Passage, Spitalfields, London E. d: 12 July 1940 in Brighton.
..+ Jean Conway b: 23 March 1870 in Glasgow d: 03 May 1946 in Brighton
...**2** David Gold b: 19 January 1895 in London d: 10 March 1970 in Edgware General Hospital, Middlesex
...**2** Susan Gold b: 27 September 1897 in London d: 02 May 1978 in London
..+ Peter Marks b: 14 May 1893 in Norwich d: 27 March 1969 in London
......**3** David Marks b: 7 March 1917 in Hendon d: 30 September 1989 in Colchester
(fictitious information given in the details above)

Suggested reading: Joan Ferris Curran et al. *Numbering your Genealogy*: Basic systems, complex systems and international kin. Published by the National Genealogical Society. Special publication - No. 64 (Arlington, 2000).

Richard A. Pence. *Numbering Systems in Genealogy.* Published by the National Genealogical Society. Revised 1995.

You have acquired all the names of your family, so how do you draw your tree?

DRAWING YOUR TREE BY HAND
This may be the simplest answer if you only have two or three generations to write down, but the further back and wider you go, the more awkward it will become. You will probably need a piece of paper or graph paper which will be large enough to include four generations. Children are usually shown left to right with the eldest child being shown on the left. Therefore begin with yourself and work backwards.

Always use a pencil to write in the names so you can then erase them and replace them with the correct entry in ink. Remember to write the name of the family on the top of the sheet and the date it was compiled, e.g. Descendants of Jacob Vandermolen – 2 July 1998.

PURCHASING A PRINTED TREE
If you are not artistic or feel it is too much trouble to write your family tree from scratch, the Society of Genealogists sell ready to fill in trees in all different sizes and it is only a matter of filling in the details. Unfortunately, these charts limit you to recording a specified number of generations.

COMPUTERISED TREES
It is far easier to use a computer for drawing your family tree as you can store information on numerous generations and then print them out. There are many family tree software packages on the market, for example, *Brother's Keeper, Family Tree Maker, Roots, DoroTree* and many more. DoroTree will write in Hebrew if you wish to record the Hebrew names of your family. You will find a selection of genealogical software demonstrated at Family History Fairs, adverts and reviews in genealogical magazines e.g. *Family Tree Magazine, Family History Monthly* etc. Before deciding on any software, it is well worth looking round to see what is on the market and how prices compare.

Once you have acquired the package you feel will suit your needs, then it is time to start entering all the details of your family.

With family tree software one usually enters the oldest person first, followed by their children and so on.

Suggested reading: there is a tremendous amount which has been written by Peter Christian and David Hawgood on this subject.

The following two examples are from the *Brother's Keeper* screens – most genealogical programs will have similar information:

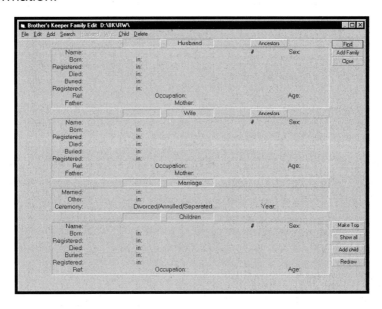

When printing out your family tree, most genealogical software packages will give you the following options:

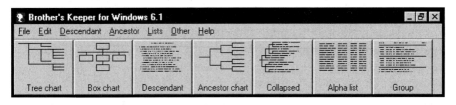

Reproduced by kind permission of John Steed (Brother's Keeper)

Photographs may be added to your trees as shown in the example below. This will help bring your tree to life and will identify the members of your family for future generations.

#147
David (Molen) Vandermolen
17 Mar 1881 - 4 Apr 1951
m. 14 Jun 1908
Miriam Barnett
31 Dec 1882 - 20 Nov 1967

There are so many more options available within these genealogical programs which will help you put your family history into some sort of order.

You may wish to:

- list the members of the family by surname
- find all the entries for a certain location
- carry out a word search
- find family birthdays and anniversaries
- produce family group sheets
- compute relationships
- produce statistics

All this and much more is possible, plus the fact the information will be produced very quickly through installing a genealogical software program and will help to organise the data you have collected.

HOW CAN I RECORD MY FAMILY HISTORY IF I DON'T HAVE ACCESS TO A COMPUTER?

If you do not have a computer and you are just going to start your family history, you might like to purchase an index card system.

Card index boxes/drawers come in various sizes. The index

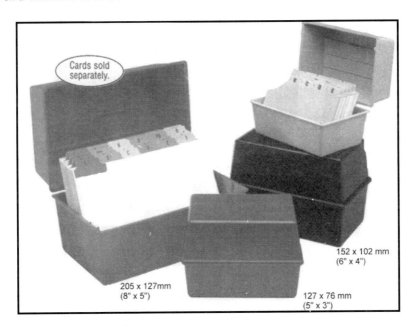

card system, as you can see from the above illustration, will help to organise your family history. If you don't want to purchase the above boxes then shoe boxes or other suitable size boxes will suffice.

Index card tabs as shown above, come in a selection of colours. Perhaps choose a different colour for each section of the family. Alphabetical/Non-alphabetical dividers are available for sale in most stationers.

You might file the index cards in alphabetical order or by a numbering system, whichever you feel would be easier. A numbering system will help you to cross-reference the cards but filing in alphabetical order will enable you to find the surnames more easily.

Bearing in mind that in the future you, or your descendants, may wish to transfer this information onto a computer, it is worth standardising the format of the cards – putting the same information in the same places.

It might be preferable to copy the information which is shown on the example of a computerised screen on page 31. The surname (in capitals), followed by the first name should be written on the top of each card. Ensure you write the details clearly and boldly so other people are able to read them easily.

NAME: GOLDSTON Isaac		INDEX CARD NUMBER: 78
	DATE	PLACE
Birth	5 April 1873	1 Sandys Row, Bishopsgate, London, E
Marriage	10 August 1897	Great Synagogue, Dukes Place, London, E
Death	20 May 1947	Paddington District (Vol.5a, Page 138)
Buried	Sec. SX. Row 5. Grave 7	Willesden Cemetery, Beaconsfield Road
RELATIVES	NAME	INDEX CARD No.
Father	Abraham Goldston	59
Mother	Amelia nee Levy	113
Spouse	Rose nee Barnett	28
Children	Alfred Goldston	79
	Agnes Goldston	80
	Leonard Goldston	81
	Marjory Goldston	82
REF Cousin John Bluestone	OTHER INFORMATION Isaac was Secretary/Minister/Reader at the New West End Synagogue from 1918 – 1946	DATE CARD PRODUCED/ UPDATED 2 March 1991 Updated 29 May 1999 Updated 14 July 2003

As with the ring-binder folder, a card index system is easy to maintain and add to as and when your family history expands. The back of the card can also be used for additional notes.

The Society of Genealogists sells both pre-printed census and genealogical record cards, (the latter are sold in packs of 50). They are 12.7cmsx10cms. The genealogical record card contains all the necessary information to document the details of births, deaths and marriages plus where they lived. The census card has room for one address with up to 12 people living at that address plus parish headings. They come in packs of approximately 70 cards. Alternatively, rather than purchasing the cards, you could design them yourself (example shown on opposite page), by putting 2 or 4 on an A4 page of thin card and photocopying them. If you wished, you could use different colour card for different sections of the family.

The index card illustrated on below left includes a space in which to enter the index card number of relatives. If you give each person in the card index a unique number, (the numbers don't have to be sequential as you will be adding new names into the system over a period of time) this will help to retrieve information quickly in a numerically ordered system; and it will guard against confusion in an alphabetically ordered system if, as in the example on page 25, lots of people have the same name.

The card shows the very basic details required. Obviously you can add anything else you like (e.g. baptism, confirmation, *Bar/Bat Mitzvah* or cemetery information).

On the computerised systems, there is a space to record who supplied the original information or where it came from (a relative, a birth, marriage or death certificate, census, book etc.) It is well worthwhile having something similar on your card index form to enable you to refer back should the need arise.

As you will see, once you get going there are a lot of boxes that you might want to put on your card index form. But the card itself it not that big, and there is a lot to be said for keeping it to basics. Anything more ought to go in proper files. A compromise might be to prepare a standard summary page (like the example shown on page 34, but fuller) that fits on a sheet of A4 then place it into an A4 ring-binder folder.

HOW TO CROSS-REFERENCE

It is essential that the index number of the named person on the card is shown on his/her parent's index cards and those of their children.

For example:

In the example shown on page 34, the father of Isaac Goldston is Abraham Goldston (index card No. 59) – on his card would be shown his wife, Amelia nee Levy (No. 113), Isaac Goldston (No. 78) and any other children together with their index numbers.

OTHER SUGGESTIONS
LABEL MAKERS

If you don't have very clear writing and do not own a computer it might be worthwhile to purchase a lettering/label system.

This will make your family history folders look very professional. There are many on the market to choose from.

The labels come in numerous colours or clear if you prefer.

HIGHLIGHTER PENS

These are always a good buy as they come in a good range of colours. There are a number of makes available, some cheaper than others. They may be purchased in a pack as the example shows or individually. On the downside, over a period of time the colours unfortunately do tend to fade.

HANDY 4-COLOUR WALLET

NOTE: When using highlighter pens, DO NOT use the dark colours e.g. pink and dark blue as they photocopy black. If you are going to highlight for example, the descendants of a person on a family tree, then draw a line with a highlighter pen under the name of the person, in this way you will ensure that when photocopied the names will remain readable.

CDs

If you have a lot of irreplaceable information, it is worth copying it digitally – if possible on to a CD or CDs, or even DVDs. All of these have high enough capacity to be able to store large numbers of photographs, and/or large numbers of direct copies of original documents. Even just storing your family tree on a CD, along with other information that is already computerised, can be very valuable as back up.

The first thing you need is a CD-writer facility on the computer you are going to use.

CD WRITERS

What do I need to write my own discs?

You will need a computer with a CD writer. A CD writer, or 'CD-RW drive', can be connected to the computer in a number of ways. The most reliable CD-RW drives are installed internally, and connected to the computer via the IDE interface. Your hard disc and existing CD-ROM use the IDE interface. If you want to add a CD-RW drive external to your computer, you can get a SCSI CD writer which attaches via a cable. However, most PCs don't have SCSI interfaces, so you have to add one by installing a PCI expansion card.

You may also find external CD writers which use the computer's parallel printer port or USB port. Although these may have some value for specialized applications (e.g., laptops), they are generally not as reliable as CD-RW drives which use the IDE or SCSI interface.

You will also need software. *Easy CD Creator* from *Roxio* is a popular choice for *Windows* users. It is included free with many CD-RW drives. If you do not have any software, or you are not happy with the software you have, you can try a shareware package like *Nero* or *CDRWIN*.

Finally, you'll need blank CD-R or CD-RW discs.

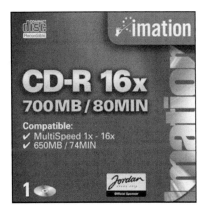 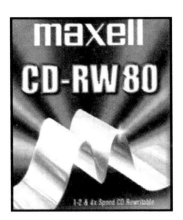

If you are simply copying existing computer files (e.g. your family tree) to the CD, you will find this process fairly straightforward. Depending on your software, it should be enough to go into *Windows Explorer*, right-click on the document that you want to copy, then left-click on 'send to', then again on 'DVD/CD-RW Drive': the rest should be self-explanatory.

If, however, you want to copy originals of documents (e.g. photographs, birth certificates etc) on to a CD, you will need a scanner, and you may also find it easier if you have some form of image manipulation software (e.g. the basic forms of *Photoshop*).

It is advisable to store scanned images with an accepted standard format readable on most computers. The most common is that devised by the Joint Photographic Expert Group, which is known as JPEG with .jpg being the file name suffix used.

ORGANISING THE ENTRIES

How then should all the documents be organised before writing to a CD?

The following example shows some possible main headings, sub-headings and in some cases another section of sub-headings

ARCHIVES

INDEXES
Address index
Birth, Marriage/Ketubot and Death indexes
Grave index

FAMILY SURNAMES
Barnett
Benjamin
Goldston
Myers
Nunes-Martines/Martin
Vandermolen/Molen
Wenzerul

Against each of the above surnames the following headings were listed:

BAR/BAT-MITZVAH

CERTIFICATES
Birth
Marriage
photographs
invitations
Ketubot
Death
Free Birth, Marriage & Death Indexes

CORRESPONDENCE
Entered as: year/month/date of each letter

GRAVES
Cemetery plans
Eulogies
Grave location cards
Photographs of graves
*Full list of all family graves (including inscriptions) in alphabetical order

MISC
Listed by surname
Family recipes
Family stories
Indexes of births, marriages and deaths
Full address lists in alphabetical order
*Full list of all family graves (including inscriptions) in alphabetical order

* same list

PHOTOGRAPHS
Listed by person

PROPERTY
Maps/Old O/S Maps
Photographs of property

WAR
Listed by person
AJEX
Medals
Regimental details
Release papers
Service book
War memorabilia
War stories

Under 'listed by person' it is worth giving a separate 'folder' to each member of the family, with a main folder for their parents. In this way, anyone looking at the information could see how the families were related. The illustration on the following page shows how this looks on the screen. Each 'folder' is indicated by a little square box. The plus sign next to a box indicates that there are sub-headings. The minus sign shows when the 'folder' is open and the sub-headings displayed.

It is also important, in the case of photographs and any other documents which, unlike birth certificates, are not self-explanatory, to annotate them in some way to show who they are or what they are about. If you do not do this, the future reader will be no wiser than looking at unidentified photographs in an album. You can do this in several ways:

- if you are collecting the images in a program such as *Word*, you can add any amount of text above or below (or over!) the image.

- if you are using *Photoshop* or a similar program, you can incorporate simple captions in the image using the 'Text' facility

- if you are working simply with *Windows* folder, 'My Pictures', you can use the file name facility.

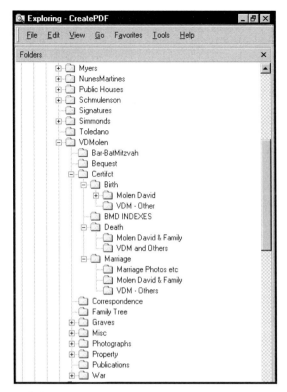

CD STORAGE

It is possible to purchase various designs of CD storage units including, racks, wallets and drawers. One of the cheapest methods is probably the rack as the example below shows.

SENDING DISCS/CDs BY POST

You may wish to send copies of the information you have collected to other members of your family. It is not worth the risk of placing these in an ordinary envelope without any protection. Although 'jiffy bags' are excellent for sending fragile items, there are, on the market specific 'mailers' for discs and CDs. The plastic ones for discs are sold in packs of five in a variety of colours and possibly are the more economical as they can be re-used.

The cardboard mailers (for discs) are for direct posting, whereas the plastic ones still have to be put into an envelope. The cardboard mailers come in packs of ten and are roughly the same price as the five plastic ones.

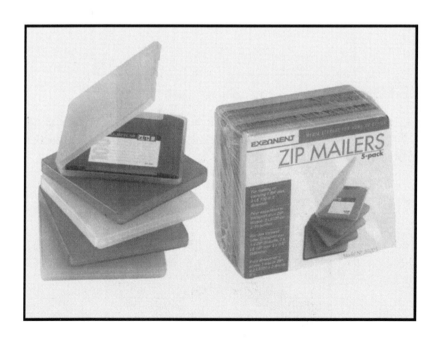

VITAL RECORDS

Whenever you acquire a birth, marriage or death certificate, ensure you extract as much information as possible from each of these documents and enter the details onto your family tree. Most genealogical software programs have sections for this information, in addition to areas set aside for notes.

Once the details have been recorded, the certificates should then be filed in a ring-binder folder. They will need to be split into different sections, use dividers for this.

The birth and death certificates are filed in strict alphabetical order by surname as the illustration for births is shown below and an index sheet placed in the front of each section for quick reference:

INDEX OF BIRTH CERTIFICATES

SURNAME	FIRST NAME
Feldman	Alice
Goldston	Agnes
Myers	Peter
Nunes-Martines	Agnes
Vandermolen/Molen	Barry
Wenzerul	Charles

The marriage certificates and *ketubot* should be filed in strict alphabetical order by the surname of the bridegroom with the bride shown next to him as illustrated below. Ensure you cross-reference the bride so that both surnames may be found easily.

INDEX OF MARRIAGE CERTIFICATES

SURNAME BRIDEGROOM	FIRST NAME BRIDEGROOM	SURNAME BRIDE	FIRST NAME BRIDE
Barnett	Baron	Nunes-Martines	Agnes
Benjamin	Moses (Maurice)	Barnett	Nancy
Davis	Derrick	Vandermolen/Molen	Evelyn
Goldston	Joseph	Levisohn	Ida
Vandermolen/Molen	David	Barnett	Miriam
Wenzerul	Samuel	Finestein	Ada

Birth, marriage and death certificates are obtainable from the Family Record Centre, 1 Myddelton Street, London, EC1R 1UW. For further information about vital records see the publication entitled *'Jewish Ancestors' A Beginner's Guide to Jewish Genealogy in Great Britain* (ISBN 0-9537669-3-4), published by the JGSGB. (Further details and order form are shown on pages 114/115 or may be ordered via the web site on: www.jgsgb.org.uk).

Having done this, you should also keep anything relating to the above filed after the certificates.

For example:

BIRTH
- Baby scan/photographs
- Baby congratulation cards
- First lock of hair
- List of your baby's first words

MARRIAGE
- Engagement and wedding invitations
- Marriage authorisation forms
- Photographs of the wedding
- Table plan

DEATH
- Photographs of the family graves
- Grave location cards
- Eulogies/Letters of condolence
- Cemetery plans

Don't forget to extract all the detail you can from any of the above documents BEFORE you file them.

FREE BIRTH, MARRIAGE AND DEATH INDEXES:
The *FreeBMD Index* is a transcription project of the General Register Office (GRO) index volumes. The Project's objective

is to provide free Internet access to the Civil Registration index information for England and Wales. The Civil Registration system for recording births, marriages, and deaths in England and Wales has been in place since 1 July 1837 and is one of the most significant single resources for genealogical research back to Victorian times. The *FreeBMD* project only contains index information for the period 1837-1983. At the time of writing this book, the database contains over 70 million records and is being updated on a regular basis. They expect the project to be completed during 2007.

The GRO indexes are shown under the following headings:

BIRTHS December 1902

Surname	First Name(s)	Age	District	Volume	Page
GOLDSTON	Leonard Isaac		Hackney	1b	401

It would be advisable to record the District, Volume and Page number against the entry in your family history folder or pencil it in on the reverse of the certificates or record it on your computer, so that if the particular certificate was damaged or you required a further copy, you would have the information readily available.

The web site is: http://freebmd.rootsweb.com/

If there are numerous members of your family listed on this web site, it is possible to download these. In this case, record the details and file the information in your folder.

This is a very useful web site which will enable you to find the index number of a specific birth, marriage or death certificate prior to your visit to the Family Record Centre. Because it is so popular, you may have difficulty in accessing it on your first attempt. Additional information may be obtained about the GRO Indexes and the other services provided by writing to the GRO, Smedley Hydro, Trafalgar Road, Southport, Merseyside, PR8 2HH and asking for a free copy of 'A Guide to our Services'.

FAMILY WEDDINGS

As with any occasion there will be numerous mementos to collect. With a marriage the following are some of the documents you may have at home:

- Engagement invitation
- Engagement gift list
- Wedding invitation
- Marriage certificate/*Ketubah* (Marriage Contract)
- List of guests/Table Plan
- Wedding gift list
- Menu
- Photographs of the Synagogue
- Photographs of the occasion
- Memorabilia from the day
- Honeymoon

The above documents all hold useful information and this should be extracted before they are filed. If you file the documents without looking at them carefully, you may miss valuable information. I cannot emphasize this enough.

Don't forget to include with your wedding memorabilia, the letters from guests who attended the wedding and in years to come letters from your Silver and Golden Wedding.

If you refer to the book entitled '*Genealogical Resources within the Jewish Home and Family*' (ISBN 1 86006 148 6), it will explain how all these documents relate to one another and will draw attention to the amount of valuable information each document contains.

Always be on the lookout for unusual signs. For instance, on the following example of a marriage certificate you will note that the bride has signed her name with an 'o' and against this it is stated – the mark of Nancy Ellis. This was because the bride couldn't read or write. Note: Jews who couldn't read or write didn't want to put a cross so they used a circle instead.

CERTIFIED COPY OF AN ENTRY OF MARRIAGE

GIVEN AT THE GENERAL REGISTER OFFICE

Application Number WO0 6503

18 69. Marriage solemnized at Flat Bradford in the Parish of District of the Place in the County of London

No.	When Married	Name and Surname	Age	Condition	Rank or Profession	Residence at the time of Marriage	Father's Name and Surname	Rank or Profession of Father
169	Third day of February 1869.	Levi Barnets	25	Bachelor	Clothier	30 Flower Street	Joshua Barnets	Clothier
		Fanny Ellis	25	Spinster		16 Flower street	Jane Ellis	Clothier

Married in the Flat Bradford according to the Rites and Ceremonies of the Jewish Religion by certificate by me

This Marriage was solemnized between us { Levi Barnets / O The mark of Fanny Ellis }

In the Presence of us { Levi Asher / Moses Misrer }

CERTIFIED to be a true copy of an entry in the certified copy of a register of Marriages in the Registration District of London City
Given at the GENERAL REGISTER OFFICE, under the Seal of the said Office, the 11th day of March 19 94

MX 743224

This certificate is issued in pursuance of section 65 of the Marriage Act 1949. Sub-section 3 of that section provides that any certified copy of an entry purporting to be sealed or stamped with the seal of the General Register Office shall be received as evidence of the marriage to which it relates without any further or other proof of the entry, and no certified copy purporting to have been given in the said Office shall be of any force or effect unless it is sealed or stamped as aforesaid.

CAUTION.—It is an offence to falsify a certificate or to make or knowingly use a false certificate or a copy of a false certificate intending it to be accepted as genuine to the prejudice of any person, or to possess a certificate knowing it to be false without lawful authority.

WARNING: THIS CERTIFICATE IS NOT EVIDENCE OF THE IDENTITY OF THE PERSON PRESENTING IT.

MARRIAGE CERTIFICATES – DESCRIPTION OF OCCUPATION

Old certificates (and census forms) often give very general descriptions (like dealer, agricultural labourer) that can only be understood properly by looking back at the instructions guiding registrars and census enumerators at the time. The terms we use today may seem clearer to us, but will still need explaining to future generations.

Agent	Land Agent, Insurance Agent, Shipping Agent
Civil Servant	Official rank to be stated followed by the name of the Department in which employed, e.g. Administrative Officer, Department of Health or Counter Clerk, Post Office
Clerk	Bank Clerk, Solicitor's Clerk, Railway Booking Clerk
Contractor	Building Contractor, Haulage Contractor
Dyer	Material to be stated, e.g. Fur Dyer, Silk Dyer
Confectioner	Confectioner and Tobacconist, Baker's Confectioner, Sweet Confectionery Shop Keeper
Engineer	Civil, Consulting and Mining Engineers and other professional engineers should also be described
Fitter	Kind of business should be indicated, e.g. Motor Fitter, Hot Water Fitter, Tailor's Fitter, Boiler Fitter
Labourer	Kind of business should be indicated, Agricultural Labourer, Building Labourer, Iron Foundry Labourer, General Labourer etc
Machine Worker	Kind of machine and nature of business should be stated, e.g. Tailor's Sewing Machinist, Milling Machinist, Cutting and Wrapping Machine Operator etc
Porter	Dock Porter, Railway Porter, Hotel Porter
Salesman	The commodity sold should be indicated, e.g. Woollen Salesman, Rainwear Saleswoman etc
Technician Technical	Any professional qualifications should be stated in addition to the kind of service or business in which the person is employed, e.g. Technical Assistant, A.M.I. Mech. E., Department of the Environment

To help you further, there is an excellent web site which lists pages and pages of old occupations:

http://www.cpcug.org/user/jlacombe/terms.html

Current guidance issued by the Registrar General for Secretaries for Marriages of Synagogues (1998) gives the above definitions, but always remember to add a note to your family records to explain occupations more clearly to succeeding generations. How many people, for example, who were born after about 1980 will have any idea what a punch-card operator was?

KETUBOT (Marriage Contracts – Jewish)

These can give a lot of further information, if you are able to read them. For example, the *Ketubah* shown on the next page, gives us a very important clue. The handwritten text indicates by the Hebrew word ארמלתא that Isabella Simmonds was a widow. In this case, looking through your family history file may bring to light the name of her first husband and the children, if any, from that marriage. Other clues which are written in Hebrew on the *Ketubah* are: בתולתא virgin/maiden, מתרכתא divorcee, גיורתא convert and חלוצתא is a childless widow no longer under an obligation to marry her husband's brother, having gone through the rite of חליצא which frees a man and woman from their obligation to perform a levirate marriage..

Don't forget to photocopy the *Ketubah* and reduce it in size to A4 so that it will fit into your folder.

Remember, *Ketubot* should be filed with the Marriage Certificate with the names of the bride and groom cross-referenced so that both surnames may be found easily.

If a person doesn't have the *Ketubah* of a deceased relative who was married in a United Synagogue and needs the details of the marriage, then the Marriage Authorisation Department of the Office of the Chief Rabbi should be contacted. It is important that the following information is given: husband's name, wife's maiden name and date married, once this information has been received, then a copy of the **marriage authorisation form** (not the *Ketubah*) will be issued.

ב אחד בשבת שלשה ימים לחדש אדר
שנת חמשת אלפים ושש מאות וששים ושבע
לבריאת עולם למנין שאנו מנין כאן בלונדון איך
ר" יחזקאל בן ר" איוב
אמר לה להרא ארמכלתא בריינדלאבת ר"

יהושע הוי לי לאנתו כדת משה וישראל ואנא
אפלח ואוקיר ואיזון ואפרנס יתיכי ליכי כהלכות
גוברין יהודאין דפלחין ומוקרין וזנין ומפרנסין לנשיהון
בקושטא ויהיבנא ליכי כסף זוזי מאתן דחזון ליכי
מדרבנן ומזוניכי וכסותיכי וסיפוקיכי ומעל לותיכי
כאורח כל ארעא וצביאת מרת בריינדלא ארמלתא
דא והות ליה לאנתו ודין נדוניא דהנעלת ליה
בין בכסף בין בזהב בין בתכשיטין במאני דלבושא
בשימושי דירה ובשימושא דערסא חמשין זקוקים
כסף צרוף וצבי ר" יחזקאל חתן דנן
ותן דנן והוסיף לה מן דיליה חמשין זקוקים
כסף צרוף אחרים כנגדן סך הכל מאה זקוקים כסף
צרוף וכך אמר ר" יחזקאל חתן דנן
אחריות שטר כתובתא דא נדוניא דן ותוספתא דא
קבלית עלי ועל ירתי בתראי להתפרע מכל שפר ארג
נכסין וקנינין דאית לי תחות כל שמיא דקנאי ודעתיד
אנא למקני נכסין דאית להון אחריות ודלית להון
אחריות כלהון יהון אחראין וערבאין לפרוע מנהון
שטר כתובתא דא נדוניא דן ותוספתא דא ואפילו מן
גלימא דעל כתפאי בחיי ובמותי מן יומא דנן ולעלם
ואחריות וחומר שטר כתובתא דא נדוניא דן ותוספתא
דא קבל עליו ר" יחזקאל חתן
דנן כחומר כל שטרי כתובות ותוספתא דנהגין
בבנת ישראל העשויין כתיקון חכמינו זכרונם לברכה
דלא כאסמכתא ודלא כטופסי דשטרי וקנינא מן
ר" יחזקאל בן ר" איוב חתן
דנן למרת בריינדלא בת ר" יהושע
ארמלתא דא בכל מה דכתב ומפורש לעיל במנא דכשר
למקניא ביה הכל שריר וקים:

Make a new section in your family history folder to file all the documentation.

DOCUMENT LINKS

Any other documents can be placed in the order in which they happened. Therefore the first document filed would be the engagement announcement, followed by the engagement invitation, marriage authorisation form, wedding invitation and so on. In this way you link up a whole series of events and this will tell the whole story of the occasion. The example on the following page illustrates this.

WEDDING EXAMPLE
DOCUMENT LINKS

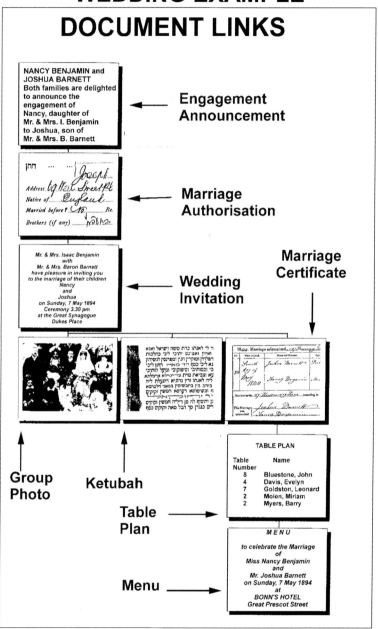

NANCY BENJAMIN and
JOSHUA BARNETT
Both families are delighted
to announce the
engagement of
Nancy, daughter of
Mr. & Mrs. I. Benjamin
to Joshua, son of
Mr. & Mrs. B. Barnett

← **Engagement
Announcement**

← **Marriage
Authorisation**

Mr. & Mrs. Isaac Benjamin
with
Mr. & Mrs. Baron Barnett
have pleasure in inviting you
to the marriage of their children
Nancy
and
Joshua
on Sunday, 7 May 1894
Ceremony 3.30 pm
at the Great Synagogue
Dukes Place

← **Wedding
Invitation**

**Marriage
Certificate**

↓

**Group
Photo** **Ketubah**

**Table
Plan** →

Menu →

TABLE PLAN

Table Number	Name
8	Bluestone, John
4	Davis, Evelyn
7	Goldston, Leonard
2	Molen, Miriam
2	Myers, Barry

M E N U

to celebrate the Marriage
of
Miss Nancy Benjamin
and
Mr. Joshua Barnett
on Sunday, 7 May 1894
at
BONN'S HOTEL
Great Prescot Street

On group photographs, ensure you name all the people in the photographs so in years to come they will be easily identifiable.

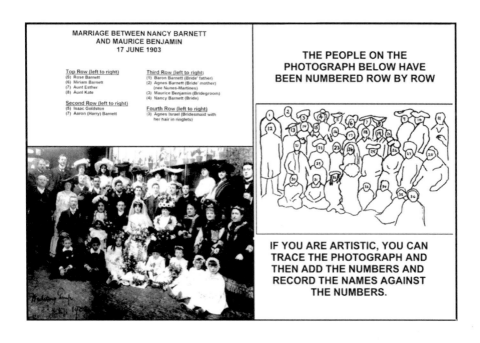

Never stick numbers or names onto original photographs in order to identify them. The above illustrates how to do this.

Once you have traced the outlines of the people in the photograph onto tracing paper, it can be photocopied or scanned onto clear laminated sheets and placed over the photograph. Or to make it even easier, slip the photograph into a plastic wallet, use a marker pen and trace around the people on the photograph, give each a number – then on a separate sheet of paper, write down the names of the people against the allocated numbers.

WHERE THE FAMILY LIVED

Just think of the numerous properties your family have lived in over the years; the schools the children went to; the places where the adults worked.

It is well worth visiting the areas where they were and photographing the streets and buildings. These can do a lot to bring your family history alive. You may have old photographs of the property and when you go back to look at it after say 80 years, you may find that it hasn't changed very much. But you might find that the area has been re-developed and unfortunately the house you are looking for is no longer there. You would not be the first family historian to arrive with your camera just as the bulldozers were moving in, and to get your photograph literally in the nick of time.

1904

1998

If you are unlucky and the building is no longer standing, then you may find pictures of a property in the local history library.

There are a number of ways to record details of properties:

- Find a map and highlight the road where your family lived. Ensure you record the name of the map, which year it was published, the page and scale. The map could be a straightforward street map or you could look at old Ordnance Survey maps. The latter will actually show the plot of land where your house stood. Always remember that street names and numbering can change, so for any older properties it is worth checking (e.g. at the local history library) that the address you have really does correspond with the map. Remember to record the old and new name of the road.

- Should you wish to publish your family history, then copyright permission must be obtained if you wish to reproduce any maps. If you are only giving copies to your family, then this isn't necessary.

- If you find the property is for sale, contact the estate agent and ask for details. There will be a photograph and description of the property and you may find there is a plan of the interior of the property included too.

- Does the property have a history which may be of interest to future generations?

- Look at old address books and extract the details from them. Make a list in alphabetical order by surname (see example on page 58).

- Always record the date when the family lived at an address so in years to come census returns may be checked.

Once you have all this information you need to make a separate folder for family property.

The photographs should be filed with a copy of each street map, details of who lived in the property plus the dates they lived there should be recorded against each entry. If you have an estate agent's details, these too should be filed next to the photograph. Current day photographs of your own property (including garden and interior) could also be included.

- Don't forget that most genealogical software programs will have the facility for including photographs, therefore you may wish to scan in photographs of where your family lived in addition to photographs of the persons concerned.

Some of the details you will have acquired will have been taken from birth, marriage and death certificates plus old address books and census returns and should be recorded as the example below illustrates. Whether or not you know the year or the whole date this should be recorded; small details that may not be of interest to you now may prove invaluable to you, or later generations, in future research.

The address list should be recorded in strict alphabetical order by surname with the following details shown:

PERSON	ADDRESS	DATE
Barnett, Baron Barnett, Agnes Barnett, Rosetta	9 Harrow Alley, London, E.1	1896
Barnett, Baron	12½ Artillery Passage, London, E.1	12 May 1900
Goldston, Abraham Goldston, Amelia	1 Sandys Row, London, E.1	7 July 1913
Goldston, Isaac Goldston, Rose Goldston, Marjory	10 St. Petersburgh Place, Bayswater, London, W.2	1918-1946
Vandermolen, David	56 New Road, Mile End, London, E	17 March 1881
Vandermolen, David Vandermolen, Miriam Vandermolen, Barry Vandermolen, Betty	74 Dames Road, Forest Gate, London, E	17 June 1917

Obviously other members of the family lived at these addresses too, so their details should also be added. If these are unknown, they may be checked on the census returns as and when published (see page 62).

In the past, most shopkeepers and owners of small businesses lived above the premises. The photograph below is of the Admiral Keppel Public House, 77 Fulham Road, London, which was bombed during the war. Should you acquire a visiting card with the address of the premises concerned, then they should be filed together.

TEL. : KENSINGTON 0341

D. Molen

The Admiral Keppel,
77 Fulham Road, S. W. 3

While on the subject of visiting cards, you may come across a number of these relating to an individual person, these may show his/her position in a Company. The cards may indicate how this person has progressed. For example he/she could have gone from an assistant manager to a manager to an executive etc. If this is the case, the cards might be filed in the order of progression.

Unfortunately, visiting cards do not indicate dates, so they will not identify how long it took your ancestor to reach their peak position, but at least it will give you an idea of whether their career was one that progressed or was mainly static.

You may discover an old shop order form as shown on the following page. If this is a member of your family, as I have said above, they may well have lived above the premises.

Note that the shop owner has a son, what was his name? Did he have any other children? Were the family related to you, if so, how? By finding out this information it will bring this very insignificant piece of paper to life. Notice the date on the form shows they were at this address during the 1960s as indicated by 196____. Always look at documents very carefully. Trade directories can also be consulted.

The details from this form should be recorded and the form filed.

CUNningham 1457

JOHN LEVY & SON

Member of the Master Baker Company

920 Manchester Avenue,
Maida Vale, London, W.9

M _____

_____

_____   *196* __

Always go back to the address and see if the building still stands. If so, take a photograph for your folder. Ensure you record the full address, the date taken and keep the form and the photograph together.

CENSUS

Although this book is about preservation and filing, it is important not to forget to look at the census.

The census was taken every 10 years since 1801, except in 1941. The census years of relevance to genealogists are 1841-1901. This is because the earlier censuses lack individual names and the later ones are closed for 100 years.

Although searching the census might look daunting, remember that the population of Great Britain was considerably smaller in the 19th century. It was only 38 million in 1901 and only 20 million in 1851.

The Public Record Office (PRO) publication entitled, '*Making use of the Census*' gives useful information about using the census plus information about the forms and the questions asked for all the censuses from 1841 to 1901. It emphasises that an address is required to be able to search in the indexes. Where you are using a database or internet facility this is not always necessary. There are some places where the records were not preserved: the advice given is to search an earlier or later census if that is the case.

The 1901 census has been transcribed, computerised and is available online. In order to see a print of the page from the internet there is a charge. It is worth doing a surname search first so that you can narrow down the choice of pages. The 1901 census asked for birthplace, nationality, activity (whether employed, or apprentice, employment status, occupation and workplace) which was restricted to those carrying on a trade or working at home. People were also asked about whether they were deaf, dumb, blind or lame.

When searching, try as many variants of a surname as possible if you do not immediately find what you are searching for.

PHOTOGRAPHY

Photographs can be a problem if stuck into albums with no information on them whatsoever. When the family find them after many years, they are thrown away as nobody can identify them. It is, therefore, so important to catalogue your photographs, ideally as you finish a reel of film.

There are three ways of doing this:

- by writing underneath (or on the reverse) of each photograph in your album the name of the person/s the date and place taken.
- by scanning the photographs onto a program such as *Adobe Photoshop* and then adding text to each photograph, or incorporating them into a word processing document.
- by adding photographs onto your family tree – some genealogical software programs can do this. Obviously the photographs would have to have been scanned first.

By doing this, future generations will be able to identify their ancestors and the images will be kept.

I would suggest that the information is then transferred onto a CD so that copies may be given to the family (see section on the preservation of documents and photographs plus the section entitled CD.)

In addition, you may find that some of your photographs illustrate a family story. In this case, keep the photograph and the story together and ensure the photograph is referred to in the text.

Perhaps your relatives have old photographs which can be identified, but unfortunately, have been stuck into albums, and therefore, would be impossible to remove without damage, and the negatives are long gone – in this case, you don't need to spend a lot of money on having them copied professionally. It is quite easy to re-photograph them in situ at home especially if you have a reflex camera, (which shows in the viewfinder more or less exactly what you will get on your negative), fitted with a close-focusing lens. If you are able to do this yourself, it is cheaper to use colour film and process it locally, rather than purchasing black and white film, unless you are in a position to print it yourself. Some photographic processing laboratories will give you the option of supplying your photographs onto a CD as well as your prints.

In addition, one should index both old and new negatives. Books to keep negatives (as I have mentioned earlier) may be purchased from most camera shops. I would recommend that when you have your prints processed, that you ask the shop NOT to cut your negatives (which they would otherwise do into 4 per row). This allows you to cut them yourself into six per row which is the size that the negative filing strips are prepared for. Remember, negatives should be stored in a cool, dry, dark place. If you haven't got a reasonable camera, but have a computer with a flatbed scanner, you can use this to copy your photos instead.

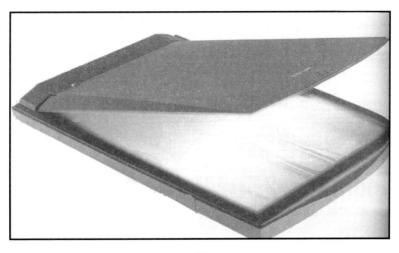

SCANNERS

There are many types of scanners on the market. To enable you to scan anything from family photographs to your grandfather's medals, the use of a flat bed scanner will do the trick. Most low cost desktop flatbed scanners have a maximum optical resolution of between 300-600 dpi.

Whilst a number of flatbed scanners have facilities for scanning negatives or transparencies (slides - this can only be done if they have a light in the lid), if you are intending to scan large numbers of 35mm negatives or slides it may be worthwhile buying a specialist scanner such as *Nikon Coolscan*, *Minolta* or *Canon*.

A scanner will enable you to crop unnecessary additions to your photographs.

In addition, some scanners have a lid which will adjust and edge glass platens for book photocopying, where the book folds over the edge and only has to open 90-120°.

PHOTOGRAPH YOUR RELATIVES

Remember, if you meet a new member of your family, whom you have found through your research, or by any other means, ensure you take a photograph of them, record their name and the date taken. Nowadays, it is easy to scan the print and e-mail it around to other relatives or interested parties. In addition check that you have up-to-date photographs of your immediate family.

Ensure you write a note saying to which part of the family he/she is connected and what other parts of the family they are researching.

If you know the maiden name, ages or dates of birth of the people in the photographs, include this information as well.

By recording the ages of any children on photographs, this will illustrate how they change with age. Children may bring home photographs they have had taken each year at school – ensure the dates are put onto these and if there is no indication of the school, include details and file them in age or date order or scan them into your system.

REFLECTIONS AND SHADOWS

If you are taking a photograph through glass and you find you have a reflection, by using a polarising filter on your camera it will help to minimise the reflection; or else change the angle of the photo to the light falling on it.

If your subject is in shadow, then a piece of white card or special 'reflectors' placed near to it will help reflect the light onto the area concerned.

DIGITAL PHOTOGRAPHY

Digital cameras will do almost anything that a conventional camera will do and, of course, quite a number of things which they cannot do. For instance, a digital camera will take photographs which can then be sent by e-mail to friends or family. In addition, each photograph you take you can view before saving it.

Digital cameras do not take conventional rolls of film; instead they have a form of electronic memory, usually in one of a number of types of removable card. This enables the photographer to down-load the images directly to the computer rather than having to have the film developed. The most common types of memory card are *CompactFlash*, *SmartMedia* and *Memory Stick*. Memory cards come in various densities, therefore you must ensure you use the correct card for your digital camera.

When buying a digital camera ensure it is the correct one which will meet all your needs.

For example check that the camera has:

- the right resolution
- enough memory and the correct lens
- the design features required (eg size and weight)

In addition check on how long the batteries will last. The price will vary according to the quality and facilities of the camera.

If you are stuck as to which camera to choose, then there are many photographic and digital photographic magazines on the market. Better still, visit a specialist photographic store such as Jessops (web site: http://www.jessops.co.uk) – they will be able to show you the cameras and explain all the design features to you.

BASIC CAMERAS
Modern technology is very expensive and there is no reason whatsoever why you shouldn't continue to use your conventional camera. Having said this, obviously it will not have all the facilities on offer from SLRs or Digital cameras, but you will still be able to produce a reasonable print.

BAR/BAT MITZVAH

In the Jewish Religion, a boy has his *Bar Mitzvah* on reaching the age of 13 and a girl her *Bat Mitzvah* at the age of 12.

It is a good idea prior to your *Bar/Bat Mitzvah* to record on tape the portion you will read from the Torah. This will bring back memories of the day you became a young man or woman. By recording your portion on a good quality tape it may have better sound quality and will last longer.

Remember after recording to <u>remove</u> the tabs on the tape cassette so that the tape isn't accidentally overwritten.

Perhaps make additional copies for other members of your family.

Remember to include oral testimonies from your parents or grandparents about their *Bar/Bat Mitzvah*.

Don't forget your party. Photographs will be taken of the event. Ensure you record the names of the people on the photographs and if you write about the day's events, perhaps you can mention how the people on the photographs are related to you. On the tables at your party, perhaps you will have *Kippot* and benching books with your name and the date of your *Bar/Bar Mitzvah* printed inside them – there will be the table plan and the menu with the names of the people giving the various toasts – all this information is so important to keep.

All these documents should be filed under a separate heading in your family history file.

If you keep the invitation, in years to come, you may find that you have your *Bar/Bat Mitzvah*, engagement and wedding invitations. These will all link up various stages of your life. (Please see section on Document Links on page 97)

MEMORIES

It is important to record your memories – they could include your childhood, schooldays, teenage years, Bar/Bat Mitzvah, engagement and marriage, stories and experiences about the war, special events, popular music/pop idols, fashion of the day which includes not only clothes but what hairstyle you had plus the design of shoes you wore etc.

CHILDHOOD/SCHOOLDAYS

A new section of your folder should be opened with the details of your childhood, schooldays and teenage years plus the memories relating to these. Keep them in the order in which they happened. Remember to include as many dates as possible.

The following is a list of items you may have collected relating to your schooldays and teenage years

- uniform price-list

- school reports

- certificates and awards

- games played at school

- childhood memories

- birthday parties

If you played games at school or at home, there may have been rhymes put to these games, therefore keep a note of these.

Note the differences between when you were a child and perhaps when your parents or grandparents were children:

To those growing up in the early 1950s birthday parties were wonderful. In those days traditional party games and food were provided e.g. pass the parcel, musical chairs, blind man's buff, pin the tail on the donkey.

The food, (rationing was still in place – do you still have your ration books?) would have been dainty little cut sandwiches with the crusts taken off, jelly in little frilly paper containers and of course, the birthday cake – nobody had bouncy castles although you may have had a conjuror or a Punch and Judy show.

Girls used to wear short dresses with rosebuds or smocking on them, short puffed sleeves plus a large bow at the back – they were so pretty. In addition, girls wore bows in their hair which would match the bow on their dress. Boys were in short trousers and as you will see from the photograph below they sometimes wore ties or bow ties. Therefore if you have a photograph of yourself as described keep it with the information and file it under this section.

SCHOOLDAYS

Ask your parents or grandparents to tell you about their first day at school and write it down.

You may come across your ancestors' school reports. Keep the reports in date order. Look at them and see what subjects they were good or bad at, which school they went to and the year, the name of the teacher, how many pupils were in the class and their position in class. Make a note of the schools they attended and the dates. Then file the report with the other details from your school.

LONDON COUNTY COUNCIL
ESSENDINE JUNIOR SCHOOL

REPORT FOR YEAR ENDING 22nd July 19 55.

Name Rosemary M Lea   Number in Class 39

Class 2nd Year Juniors.   Position in Class 4th

SUBJECT		ASSESSMENT	REMARKS
ENGLISH	Reading	Excellent	Rosemary has worked hard
	Composition	Very good	
	Comprehension	Good	Keeness to write much
	Spelling	Very good	often destroys her grammar.
ARITHMETIC		Good	A great improvement.
HISTORY		Fair	Inclined to wander.
GEOGRAPHY		Good	Good, keen work.
SCIENCE		Good	
ART		Good	Very good work
WRITING		Good	Erratic. Could be excellent.
HANDWORK (Needlework)		Fair	
OTHER SUBJECTS	Nature Study	Good	A good year's work.

RELIGIOUS KNOWLEDGE Good   Attendance Excellent

GENERAL REPORT
Rosemary has worked hard throughout the year and progressed well. With persistent effort she should further improve next year. Her conduct is excellent

Class Master   A·E·King   Head Master

HISTORICAL MOMENTS

Family history should be about more than your immediate family, or it will come across as flat and narrow to people reading about it later on. It will come alive if you are able to weave in details of any historical moments in your life, for example:

- Death of King George VI
- Queen Elizabeth II Coronation
- First man on the moon
- Death of Princess Diana
- Millennium
- September 11 2001 –Twin Towers, New York, USA
- Death of Queen Elizabeth the Queen Mother
- Queen Elizabeth II Golden Jubilee (or Silver Jubilee)
- Other disasters or events which may have involved your own family (World Cup/Olympics etc)

All the above events will have been recorded by historians and will be written down in the history of our country and recorded in the newspapers of the time. However, it will be far more interesting for future generations to read a page or so of their own family's reactions, thoughts and emotions and to know that they actually lived through these events. If you are not sure exactly what to write about, the following example will help you:

Queen Elizabeth II Golden Jubilee:
Queen Elizabeth II's Accession to the throne was on 6th February 1952.
The Golden Jubilee celebrations included Street parties, the two concerts at Buckingham Palace, the wonderful fireworks, were you lining the streets to St. Paul's Cathedral when the Coronation coach came by? Did you watch everything on television (the BBC televised the occasion in over 40 countries)? What did you think of the magnificent carnival? Were any of your family in the procession? (Mention was made of the Jewish Lads' and Girls' Brigade). What did you

think of the Queen's two stunning outfits? Were you moved by seeing so many people singing Land of Hope and Glory and waving flags when the Royal Family appeared on the balcony? The fly-pass of Concorde and the Red Arrows. Maybe you spoke to a member of the Royal Family.

These are just a few ideas which you could write about.

If you took any photographs at the time, include these. By illustrating the text, you will bring the whole document to life. In case you are not aware, you can take very successful photographs directly from the television screen with a basic camera. Do NOT use flash as it will destroy the image. When the photographs have been developed, keep them in order, say what each photograph depicts and include the date taken, unless you have this facility on the camera and the date is printed onto the photograph. File these in the designated section of your family history file, or produce a collage on your computer.

Don't forget to mention the names of the family and friends who were with you on the day and ensure you record the date the events took place. In addition, put your name at the bottom of the article. In years to come, future generations will be able to identify the name of the person who wrote the article with the name and date of the event.

Writing down your thoughts will only take about half-an-hour of your time, so please make the effort immediately after any significant national, personal or family event has taken place.

ROMANTIC MEMORIES

If a close relative had a love of a specific flower, pick one or two and press them (or scan them!) and put these into your family history file. Don't forget to record the name of the person and, of course, the name of the flower, as sometimes the flowers are rather unrecognisable when pressed. Did they connect the flower to an event in their lives?

The flower below is Orange blossom/Syringa and whenever my father (Barry Molen) came to my home he would always remark on the smell of these flowers when he walked into the garden as they brought back memories of Italy during the Second World War. Presumably, the flowers were growing there at that time.

Valentine cards or 'love letters' – these too will bring back memories of the love and romance which came into your life.

A special gift received from a loved one – for example one red rose or a surprise trip on the Orient Express to Paris – keep the tickets or other memorabilia.

All these memories should be recorded for future generations to cherish, therefore file them together in a section of your folder.

UNIVERSITY OR COLLEGE

This for many people is the next important stage of their lives.

Keep your details and those of your parents', brothers' and sisters' degree ceremonies, along with their certificates and photographs. These should all be filed in a separate section of your folder in the order they happened.

Graduation

Don't forget, after the ceremony to write about the day's events.

Perhaps you have found out that a relative went to a particular college or university. It is well worth writing to them requesting information.

UNIVERSITY OF LONDON

Presentation of Graduates to

The Rt Hon The Lord Flowers

The Vice-Chancellor

The Royal Albert Hall

Wednesday 4 December 1985

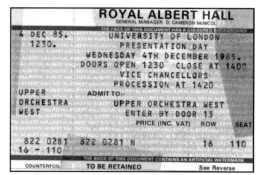

ROYAL ALBERT HALL
GENERAL MANAGER: D. CAMERON McNICOL

THE FACE OF THIS DOCUMENT HAS A COLOURED BACKGROUND

4 DEC 85.
1230.

UNIVERSITY OF LONDON
PRESENTATION DAY
WEDNESDAY 4TH DECEMBER 1985.
DOORS OPEN 1230 CLOSE AT 1400
VICE CHANCELLORS
PROCESSION AT 1420

UPPER
ORCHESTRA
WEST

ADMIT TO:

UPPER ORCHESTRA WEST
ENTER BY DOOR 13

PRICE (INC. VAT)   ROW   SEAT

822 0281 822 0281 N   16   110
16 - 110

THE BACK OF THIS DOCUMENT CONTAINS AN ARTIFICIAL WATERMARK

COUNTERFOIL   TO BE RETAINED   See Reverse

Make a note of the names of your colleagues at university and the year you knew them. If you have photographs of them, ensure you note their names and date against the photograph.

If you haven't got a copy of the University or College prospectus, write and ask for one. It may have photographs of the buildings or communal areas you remember and would be worth keeping with your other documents.

The same applies for student accommodation. It might be interesting to take a photograph of this and write about your flatmates, how near you were to the University or College, what facilities you had etc. In years to come, you will be able to reminisce on your student days.

Any information you extract or receive should be recorded and the documents filed.

NATIONAL SERVICE

Did any of your family serve in the forces?

There are so many documents and memorabilia relating to National Service. Whether your family served in the Army, Navy or Air Force they are bound to have kept memorabilia – for example:

- Service ID number/Regiment
- Call-up papers
- Soldier's Service and Pay Book
- Soldier's Release Book
- Release Leave Certificate
- List of Campaign Stars, Clasps and Medals
- Letters from family
- Stories about war experiences
- Commonwealth War Graves Commission details
- Photographs of the family in uniform
- Special Regimental Dinners
- Maps showing where the fighting took place
- Regimental Old Comrades Association
- Insignia and Regimental badges
- Regimental journals
- Newspaper articles

There are many, many more documents which you may find within your family.

Extract as much information from them as possible and then file them in a separate section of your family history folder. Title the outside of the folder '1914-1918 and 1939-1945 Wars.' File them in the order of events.

If you visit your local public library, you will find books on the medals of the first and second world wars. There will be details against each medal showing why they were won as the illustration below indicates. In addition, there are web sites which will give you this information as well.

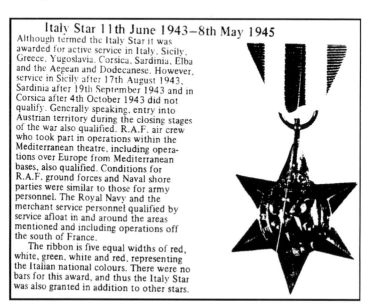

Italy Star 11th June 1943–8th May 1945

Although termed the Italy Star it was awarded for active service in Italy, Sicily, Greece, Yugoslavia, Corsica, Sardinia, Elba and the Aegean and Dodecanese. However, service in Sicily after 17th August 1943, Sardinia after 19th September 1943 and in Corsica after 4th October 1943 did not qualify. Generally speaking, entry into Austrian territory during the closing stages of the war also qualified. R.A.F. air crew who took part in operations within the Mediterranean theatre, including operations over Europe from Mediterranean bases, also qualified. Conditions for R.A.F. ground forces and Naval shore parties were similar to those for army personnel. The Royal Navy and the merchant service personnel qualified by service afloat in and around the areas mentioned and including operations off the south of France.

The ribbon is five equal widths of red, white, green, white and red, representing the Italian national colours. There were no bars for this award, and thus the Italy Star was also granted in addition to other stars.

Once you have acquired this information, there are other books available which show the battlefields, borrow these from the library and incorporate the details with your family history.

If you have photographs of your family in uniform, note against the photograph their name, rank, serial number and, if you know where they served, add this too. Perhaps there are photographs of the family taken then and now.

If you visit any Military Cemeteries belonging to the Commonwealth War Graves Commission, you will find a list of the servicemen, a plan of the cemetery (which can always be photographed) and details of the battle. Photograph the plan and mark where your relative is buried as shown on the following page:

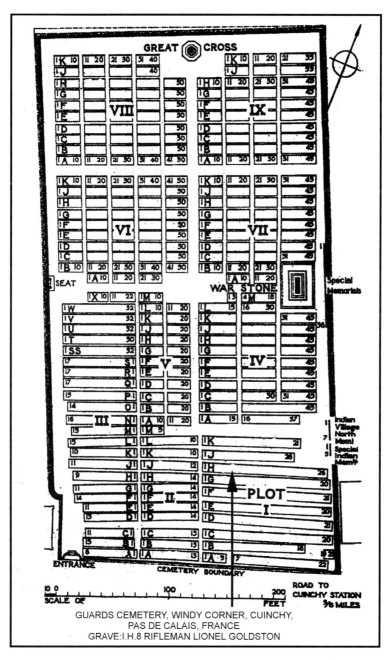

GUARDS CEMETERY, WINDY CORNER, CUINCHY,
PAS DE CALAIS, FRANCE
GRAVE:I.H.8 RIFLEMAN LIONEL GOLDSTON

Reproduced by kind permission of the Commonwealth War Graves Commission

79

The cemetery plan should be filed near to a photograph of the grave and if you have a photograph of the soldier include this too as the example below illustrates. By filing these together, it brings a section of your family history together and will tell a story. In addition on the Commonwealth War Graves Commission web site (www.cwgc.org) you will find historical details of the battle in which your relative was killed. In addition the CWGC web site also gives details of civilians killed by enemy action.

2130 Rfn. Lionel Emanuel Goldston
21st Bn., London Regt (First Surrey Rifles)
died 30 May 1915 aged 19
Buried: Guards Cemetery, Windy Corner, Cuinchy, Pas de Calais, France
Grave Reference: I.H.8
Son of Nehemiah and Floretta Goldston

Were any of your family killed during the First World War? If so, their next of kin would have received a medallion known as a "dead man's penny" – the reverse of this medallion was blank. Each medallion had the name of the deceased person. As shown below, this medallion can be scanned and kept with the accompanying papers.

Reproduced by kind permission of Mrs. June Jones

This letter accompanied the medallion on the previous page.

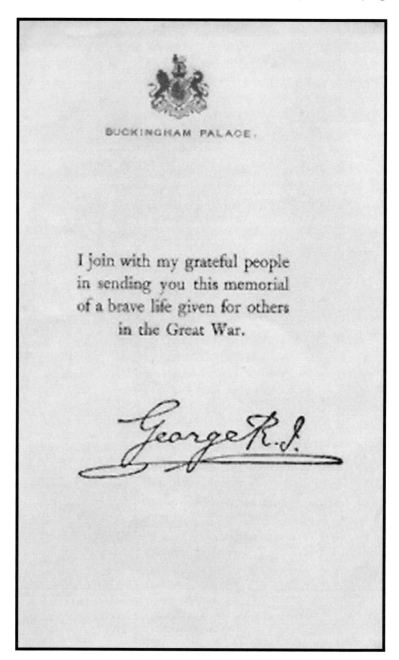

BUCKINGHAM PALACE.

I join with my grateful people
in sending you this memorial
of a brave life given for others
in the Great War.

George R.I.

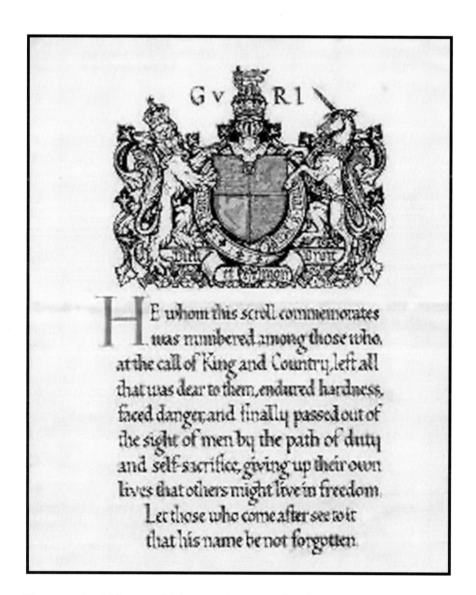

The next of kin would have also received a telegram notifying them of the death. All these documents should be filed together in your family history folder under the section – War.

BEREAVEMENT

As in their lives there will be a great deal of valuable information to collect and store about your family, so it should be after their deaths.

Indeed information collected around the time of death – a copy of the death announcement and the letters of condolence all help the bereaved to come to terms with their loss. The same documentation will be both poignant and informative to later generations.

For each member of the family who has died, try to record at least the basic information like date of death, cause of death and place of burial (or cremation).

The will should give you all sorts of information and again a copy should be filed together with the death certificate. If there are lots of people included in the will, ensure you record how they are related to you or to the deceased.

Some wills will give addresses, therefore make a note of these and note against each entry where the information was taken from and the date. Note: there is a tremendous amount of information obtainable from looking at wills.

VISITING CEMETERIES
It is important to document your family graves. The most effective way is by photographing the headstone. Some cemeteries do not allow this, so please check first with the cemetery office. It is advisable to visit the cemetery at different times of the day so you can decide when the light is at its best. If the grave is in shadow then the use of a reflector may be required.

The ideal camera would be a 35mm SLR with either a basic 50-55mm lens or a wider angle (e.g. 35mm) lens. Obviously a digital camera would be fine too. Even if you have a basic camera it is possible to take a photograph but obviously it will not give you such a good definition of the inscription.

If the headstone is unreadable, then be very careful if you attempt to improve the quality of the lettering of the inscription. Some of the very old headstones are made of sandstone and are probably impossible to read as the inscriptions on sandstone tend to erode very quickly. With other stones, a very soft brush or natural sponge and water will help to remove surface soil. Gentle brushing should remove surface dirt and bird droppings. Whatever you do, never use hard objects or stiff brushes. Better still ask the Cemetery office to arrange to clean the stone for you.

Notice how headstones made of sandstone erode

When you have taken your photographs make a note of:

- the person's English and Hebrew names

- the location
  (cemetery name, section, row and grave number)

- the date and time photographed

- the inscription on the headstone

Recording the time will help if your photograph does not come out well. It will remind you to choose a different time to re-visit to get the light right. Future generations may find it of use if the photograph no longer exists and they need to re-visit the cemetery to re-take it.

If you do not have your records on the computer, then I would suggest that you make an index card up for each person as shown below:

Name: VANDERMOLEN Betsy   **Cemetery:** East Ham Plashet

Section	Row	Grave No.	Date/Time Photograph Taken	Headstone Inscription
N	23	1	11 May 2003 10.30 am	In loving memory of Betsy, Widow of the Late Jacob Vandermolen. Late of Middlesex Street who died at 50c Romford Road March 11 1914. Aged 71. Peace to her soul. Grave also says: *Darling children I could no longer stay, the voice of G-d has called me away, I'm free from care, free from pain and trust in G-d to meet again.* Her Hebrew name was not shown on the headstone.

The cards should obviously be filed in alphabetical order.

Ask at the cemetery office for a plan of the cemetery showing the section numbers and mark where the grave is located. In this way, future generations will be able to locate the grave without any difficulty.

The cemetery plan below has been downloaded from the United Synagogue web site on:

www.unitedsynagogue.org.uk/burial.html

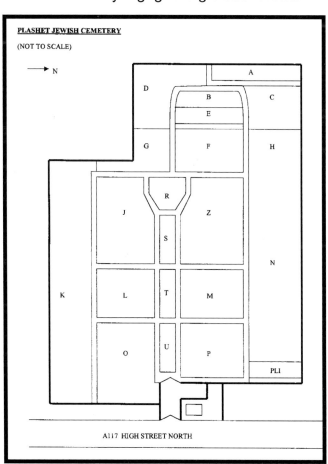

Reproduced by kind permission of the Burial Society of the United Synagogue

Cemeteries will also issue a grave location card to the family when someone dies. This should be filed in this section and the following details extracted (Cemetery Name, Section, Row, Grave Number and date of Interment).

Out of interest, note that trolley buses were still running in this area.

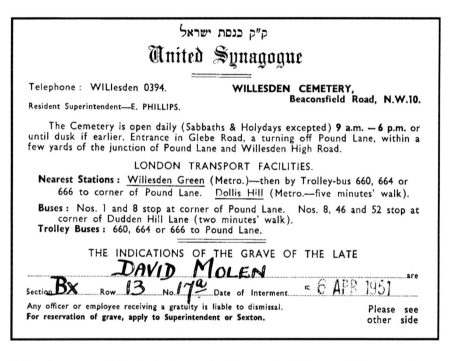

It is also sensible to take a photograph of the whole cemetery for reference from a suitable viewpoint.

You may find that some of the very old headstones actually give the address of the deceased. This is extremely useful and obviously should be recorded in your list of addresses. In this case it is important to note the source.

A copy of the text of such a headstone is shown on the following page:

In loving memory of
AGNES (nee Nunes-Martines)
widow of
BARON BARNETT
of 9 Harrow Alley, E

WHO DEPARTED THIS LIFE
30 January 1909
Aged 57

DEEPLY MOURNED BY HER
LOVING CHILDREN,
GRANDCHILDREN, GREAT
GRANDCHILDREN,
RELATIVES AND FRIENDS

MAY HER DEAR SOUL REST
IN EVERLASTING PEACE

CORRESPONDENCE

Over the years, you will have corresponded with an enormous number of researchers. Whatever you do, DON'T throw away the letters or any scrap paper you may have written down notes on.

There are two ways of dealing with them:

- file in strict alphabetical order by the surname of the researcher and then in date order.

- file by the surname of the family you are researching.

It is very worthwhile, from time to time, to re-look at old correspondence and documents as you may have acquired additional information. By looking back at previous letters, you may well find clues and information which have gone un-noticed and will, once again, point you in the right direction.

Instead of using a hole punch for each piece of paper, I would suggest you file them in plastic sleeves so it is very quick to find them within your folder and the letters will not get damaged. Ensure they are filed and kept in date order with the most recent at the top and include copies of your replies.

Perhaps include an index sheet at the front of the folders with the names of the researchers and which surnames they are researching. You may find that you have three or four people researching one surname. This system will make life a lot easier to identify them, for example:

RESEARCHER	RESEARCHING
GOLD Barry	Barnett, Bluestone, Goldston
HARRIS Janet	Goldston, Nunes-Martines
HOLDEN Susan	Barnett, Cohen, Vandermolen
MORRIS David	Barnett, Moses, Moss, Rose

Alternatively, list the names you are researching in alphabetical order with the researchers shown next to them or both:

RESEARCHING	RESEARCHER
BARNETT	Barry Gold, Susan Holden, David Morris
COHEN	Susan Holden
GOLDSTON	Barry Gold, Janet Harris
VANDERMOLEN	Susan Holden

The outside of your ring-binder folder might be shown as follows:

FAMILY TREE PART 7a CORRESPONDENCE A – J	FAMILY TREE PART 7b CORRESPONDENCE K – R	FAMILY TREE PART 7c CORRESPONDENCE S – Z

If you have an enormous amount of correspondence you may require more than 3 folders. By using a ring-binder folder, numbering them as shown (followed by a,b,c etc) it is easy to split the files up into additional folders whilst still maintaining the rest of your files in order.

RELIGIOUS DOCUMENTS

There are a number of religious documents you may acquire during your lifetime.

CIRCUMCISION (*B'rit Milah* - Jewish)

On the eighth day after birth, Jewish males are circumcised, in the ceremony called a *B'rit Milah*. The following is an example of the form which is completed by the *Mohel*. This form should be filed with photographs or other documentation relating to the boy's birth or babyhood. Remember to extract the details especially his Hebrew name.

AWARDS FROM HEBREW CLASSES (CHEDER) OR SUNDAY SCHOOL. These will indicate the name of the Synagogue or Church the name of the teacher or headmaster and, most important of all, the date the prize was given. Note: the two small documents shown below indicate that the family moved from Dalston to Bayswater sometime between 1915 and 1920. This information should be recorded until definite proof of when they moved is found. *Always look carefully at every piece of paper – you never know what information may come to light.*

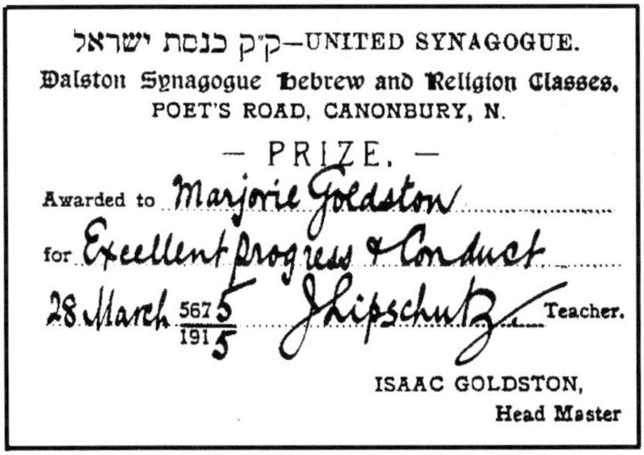

ק"ק כנסת ישראל—UNITED SYNAGOGUE.

Dalston Synagogue Hebrew and Religion Classes,
POET'S ROAD, CANONBURY, N.

— PRIZE. —

Awarded to *Marjorie Goldston*

for *Excellent progress & Conduct*

28 March 567 5
191 5   *Lipschutz* Teacher.

ISAAC GOLDSTON,
Head Master

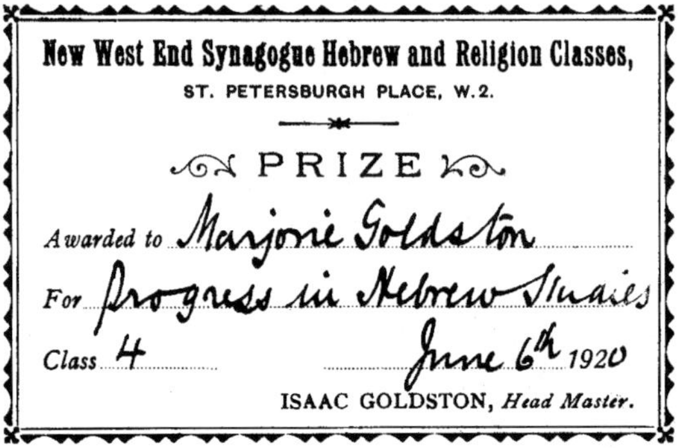

New West End Synagogue Hebrew and Religion Classes,
ST. PETERSBURGH PLACE, W.2.

PRIZE

Awarded to *Marjorie Goldston*

For *Progress in Hebrew Studies*

Class 4   *June 6th* 1920

ISAAC GOLDSTON, *Head Master.*

Copies of these inscriptions may be found on the inside pages of books and should be scanned and details of the books concerned recorded against them. Keep these in date order with your section of achievements or schooldays.

SIMCHAT TORAH (Rejoicing of the Law - Jewish)
Male members of the congregation of a Synagogue are honoured by being called to the Reading of the Law on *Simchat Torah*. They are referred to as '*Chatan Torah*' (Bridegroom of the Law) and '*Chatan Bereshit*' (Bridegroom of the Beginning). Below is an example of the certificate for *Chatan Bereshit*.
This should be filed with your achievements or with a copy of your father's or grandfather's certificates if they were given this honour.

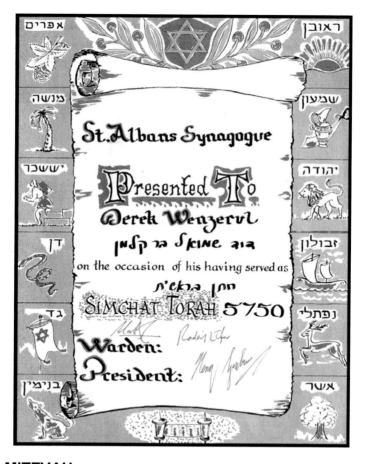

BAR-MITZVAH
See information on page 68

REFERENCES

If you have written to archives, record offices, libraries etc., it is well worth while keeping a list, in alphabetical order, of the addresses, e-mail, telephone/fax numbers and if you have them, the contacts and the date you wrote to them, so if you need to re-contact them again, it will make life a lot easier if you have a record.

RESOURCE	ADDRESS	TELEPHONE/ FAX/E-MAIL
The Jewish Genealogical Society of Great Britain	Membership Secretary JGSGB, PO Box 2508, Maidenhead, SL6 8WS	E-Mail: enquiries@jgsgb.org.uk Web site: www.jgsgb.org.uk
Jewish Historical Society of England	33 Seymour Place, London, W1H 6AT	Tel/Fax: 020 7723 5852
Hyde Park Family History Centre (Mormons)	Hyde Park FHC, Church of Jesus Christ of the Latter Day Saints, 54-68 Exhibition Road, South Kensington, London, SW7 2PA	Tel: 020 7589 8561
Royal Geographical Society	1 Kensington Gore, London, SW7 2AR	Tel: 020 7591 3000 Fax: 020 7591 3001 E-mail: info@rgs.org
Society of Genealogists	14 Charterhouse Buildings, Goswell Road, London, EC1M 7BA	Tel: 020 7251 8799 Fax: 020 7250 1800 E-Mail: genealogy@sog.org.uk
Spanish and Portuguese Jews' Congregation	2 Ashworth Road, Maida Vale, London, W9 1JY.	Tel: 020 7289 2573 Fax: 020 7289 2709

Keep copies of the pamphlets or information sheets from these organisations. These will show the opening hours and the various services they offer. If the pamphlets are not dated, then put a date on the front or back of them so when you refer to them again, you will know whether the information is relevant or out-of-date. File in alphabetical order.

MAPS

Under this section it would be a good idea to list any maps you have. For instance, there is the Alan Godfrey collection of old

Ordnance Survey maps. If you have a collection of these, list them in map number order, then which map the area covers and finally the year. This will save you the trouble of looking through all the maps for a particular copy.

Map Number	Area	Year
21	Stamford Hill	1913
30	Stoke Newington	1914
39	Highbury & Islington	1894
60	Paddington	1872
60	Paddington	1914

GENEALOGICAL MAGAZINES
If you wish to keep your old copies, file them by title and in date order into a ring-binder file. Keep the most current copy at the top. The outside label will also indicate the contents of the file.

Title	Year	Month	Vol.	No.
The Genealogist Magazine	1995	March	25	1
	1995	June	25	2
	1995	September	25	3
	1995	December	25	4
	1996	March	25	5
	1996	June	25	6
	1996	September	25	7
	1996	December	25	8
JGSGB: Shemot	2001	March	9	1
	2001	June	9	2
	2001	September	9	3
	2001	December	9	4

WEB SITE ADDRESSES
Remember to list the web sites you most frequently use – as always, these should be listed in alphabetical order and will be available as a quick reference. These sometimes change so should be checked every so often.

DOCUMENT LINKS

It is important to recognise that certain documents and photographs may relate to one another and will, therefore, provide an overall picture of a sequence of events during a person's lifetime. It is essential to look at them and re-look at them and compare them with material you have already collected in case you have missed any relevant information.

If you think of your life from beginning to end as a story and follow the various events through, one stage at a time, you will then be in a position where you can place the documents you have accumulated into some kind of order. This will enable future generations to understand and cherish the information you have collected.

The illustrations display various headings which are there to provide guidance. They demonstrate how a selection of documents and photographs link to one another. It is entirely up to each individual person to decide what information is included under the various headings and chains.

This information will help you, should you wish, to write a story with illustrations about the various events and help you keep your documents and photographs in order.

The example on page 54 illustrates the documents collected from a wedding. However, the following pages only note the headings.

As already mentioned, everyone has different documents and photographs and it is not necessary to follow the example headings shown. The illustrations are there purely as a guide and it is obviously more of a challenge for each person to gather the various documents together and make up their own links or chains of events. The main point is that the documents should be kept in order of occurrence either by date or, in the case of something like a wedding, within the day.

CHILDHOOD

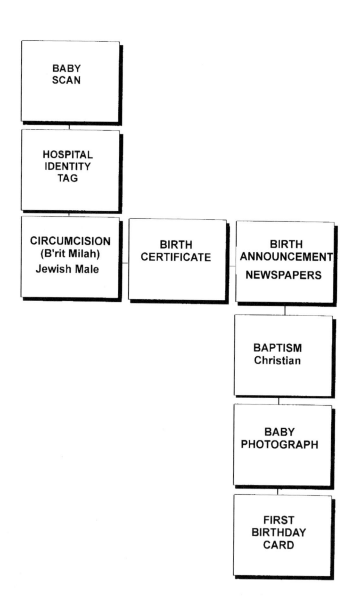

BABY
SCAN

HOSPITAL
IDENTITY
TAG

CIRCUMCISION
(B'rit Milah)
Jewish Male

BIRTH
CERTIFICATE

BIRTH
ANNOUNCEMENT
NEWSPAPERS

BAPTISM
Christian

BABY
PHOTOGRAPH

FIRST
BIRTHDAY
CARD

SCHOOLDAYS

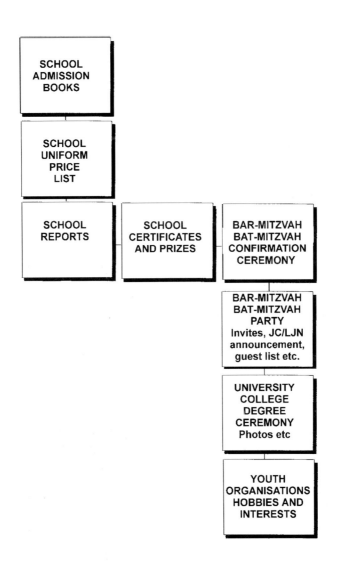

SCHOOL
ADMISSION
BOOKS

SCHOOL
UNIFORM
PRICE
LIST

SCHOOL
REPORTS

SCHOOL
CERTIFICATES
AND PRIZES

BAR-MITZVAH
BAT-MITZVAH
CONFIRMATION
CEREMONY

BAR-MITZVAH
BAT-MITZVAH
PARTY
Invites, JC/LJN
announcement,
guest list etc.

UNIVERSITY
COLLEGE
DEGREE
CEREMONY
Photos etc

YOUTH
ORGANISATIONS
HOBBIES AND
INTERESTS

WORKING LIFE

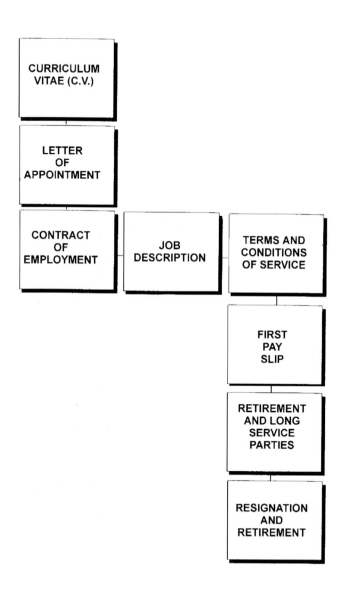

WEDDINGS

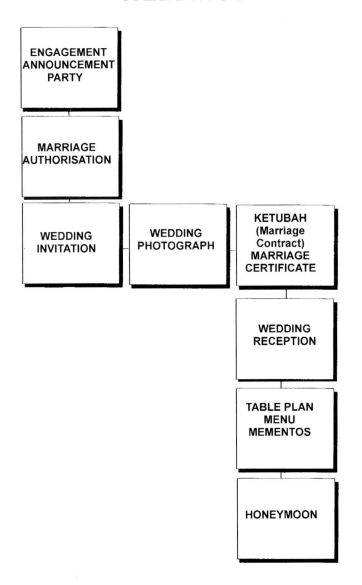

ENGAGEMENT ANNOUNCEMENT PARTY

MARRIAGE AUTHORISATION

WEDDING INVITATION

WEDDING PHOTOGRAPH

KETUBAH (Marriage Contract) MARRIAGE CERTIFICATE

WEDDING RECEPTION

TABLE PLAN MENU MEMENTOS

HONEYMOON

PROPERTY

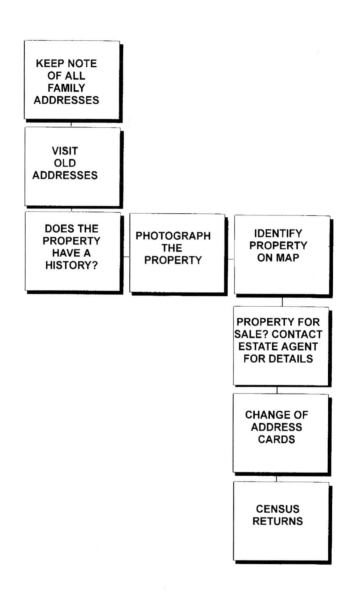

KEEP NOTE
OF ALL
FAMILY
ADDRESSES

VISIT
OLD
ADDRESSES

DOES THE
PROPERTY
HAVE A
HISTORY?

PHOTOGRAPH
THE
PROPERTY

IDENTIFY
PROPERTY
ON MAP

PROPERTY FOR
SALE? CONTACT
ESTATE AGENT
FOR DETAILS

CHANGE OF
ADDRESS
CARDS

CENSUS
RETURNS

BEREAVEMENT

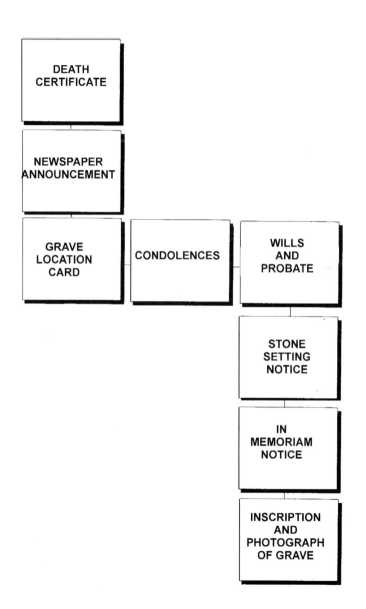

DEATH CERTIFICATE

NEWSPAPER ANNOUNCEMENT

GRAVE LOCATION CARD

CONDOLENCES

WILLS AND PROBATE

STONE SETTING NOTICE

IN MEMORIAM NOTICE

INSCRIPTION AND PHOTOGRAPH OF GRAVE

SPECIAL OCCASIONS

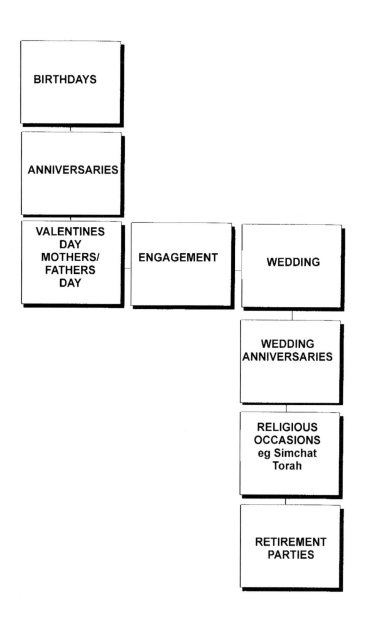

BIRTHDAYS

ANNIVERSARIES

VALENTINES DAY MOTHERS/ FATHERS DAY

ENGAGEMENT

WEDDING

WEDDING ANNIVERSARIES

RELIGIOUS OCCASIONS eg Simchat Torah

RETIREMENT PARTIES

OTHER EXAMPLES

Documents may relate to one another in more than one way. For example, individual boxes within the chain illustrations shown throughout this section may inter-link, as the following examples show:

1   You may prefer to place birth, marriage/*ketubot* and death certificates in one section rather than including them under the suggested sections. This works very well and would be easier to find if placed in alphabetical order by surname. As two names appear on a marriage certificate, I would suggest, as mentioned earlier in this book, that the certificates are filed in alphabetical order by the husband's surname and cross-referenced to the wife/bride.

2   Perhaps a section could include Valentine cards, engagement, marriage, home, children and grandchildren.

3   Maybe you would prefer to put all photographs together. This I wouldn't advise as each photograph will tell a story, therefore, splitting up your photographs within the text will add more interest to your project.

The way you decide to organise your family history is a very personal thing and although I have given you many ideas throughout this book, you may wish to design it in an entirely different way. This is fine, but do ensure that whatever you design is simple and easy for future generations to follow.

GLOSSARY

Ashkenazi(m)	From the Hebrew word for German. Ashkenazi Jews came from this region
Bar-Mitzvah	Son of the Commandments. Following a boy's 13th birthday, he is called up in the Synagogue to read a portion of the Law
Bat-Mitzvah	Usually girls have a Bat-Mitzvah at around 12 years of age
Benching Book	Grace after Meals Service
B'rit Milah	Circumcision
Chatan Bereshit	Bridegroom of the Beginning (Simchat Torah)
Chatan Torah	Bridegroom of the Law (Simchat Torah)
Haftarah	Conclusion. The portion selected from the book of Prophets and read after the Reading of the Law
Ketubah	Marriage Contract (Ketubot = plural)
Kippah	Skull Cap – also known as a Yarmulka or Koppel. (Kippot = plural)
Maftir	Concluding. The last portion of the Sidrah (see below)
Mohel	Person authorised to perform a circumcision
Sephardi(m)	From the Hebrew word for Spanish. Sephardi Jews came from this region
Siddur	Prayer Book
Sidrah	The portion of the Law read every Sabbath morning in the Synagogue
Simchat Torah	Rejoicing of the Law – 9th day of Tabernacles
Torah	5 Books of Moses - Pentateuch

ABBREVIATIONS/ADDRESSES

The following well known abbreviations in genealogy may be of help to you when filing some of your references.

GENERAL

FAMILY TREES

b	Birth
m	Marriage
d	Death
nk	Not known
c	About (e.g. c.1941)

CENSUS

H	Head of Household
Wife	Wife
Son	Son
Dau	Daughter
Unm	Unmarried
Mar	Married
Wid	Widower
Serv	Servant
Dom	Domestic

INSTITUTIONS

AJEX	Association of Jewish Ex-Service Men and Women
BOD	Board of Deputies
BT	British Telecom
FHC	Family History Centre (run by the Mormons - LDS)
FRC	Family Record Centre
GRO	General Register Office
HMSO	Her Majesty's Stationery Office
JMC	Jewish Memorial Council
LDS	Latter Day Saints (Mormons)
LMA	London Metropolitan Archives
ONS	Office of National Statistics
PCC	Prerogative Court of Canterbury
PCY	Principal Prerogative Court of York
PRO	Public Record Office – now National Archives
RAF	Royal Air Force
RGS	Royal Geographical Society

SYNAGOGUES

RSGB	Reform Synagogues of Great Britain
ULPS	Union of Liberal & Progressive Synagogues
US	United Synagogue

GENEALOGICAL

AJGS	Association of Jewish Genealogical Societies
AJHS	American Jewish Historical Society
AJHS	Australian Jewish Historical Society
CWGC	Commonwealth War Graves Commission
FTJP	Family Tree of the Jewish People
IAJGS	International Association of Jewish Genealogical Societies
IGI	International Genealogical Index
JGFF	Jewish Genealogical Family Finder
JGS	Jewish Genealogical Society
JGSGB	Jewish Genealogical Society of Greater Boston
JGSGB	Jewish Genealogical Society of Great Britain
JHSE	Jewish Historical Society of England
SIG	Special Interest Group
SOG	Society of Genealogists

NEWSPAPERS/JOURNALS

©	Copyright
ISBN	International Serial Book Number (books)
ISSN	International Standard Serial Number (periodicals)
JC	Jewish Chronicle
LJN	London Jewish News
PP	Pages
Pub	Publication
Trans	Transaction
Vol	Volume
No	Number

COMPUTERS/INTERNET

ASCII	American Standard Code for Information Interchange
DPI	Dots Per Inch
E-MAIL	Electronic Mail
GEDCOM	Genealogical Data Communication
IDE	Integrated Development Environment
ISP	Internet Service Provider
PC	Personal Computer
PCI	Peripheral Component Interconnect
PDF	Portable Document Format
RTF	Rich Text Format
SCSI	Small Computer System Interface
TIFF	Tagged Image File Forman
USB	Universal Serial Bus
WP	Word Processor
WWW	World Wide Web

PHOTOGRAPHY, CDs etc

CD-R	CD-Recordable. These discs can only be written on once.
CD-RW	CD Re-Writable. These discs can be erased allowing you to re-use them again.
DVD	Digital Video Disc
JPEG	Joint Photographic Expert Group
SLR	Single Lens Reflex

USEFUL ADDRESSES

Society of Archivists	Prioryfield House, 20 Canon Street, Taunton, Somerset, TA1 1SW. Tel: 01823 327030 Fax: 01823 371719 Email:offman@archives.org.uk
National Preservation Office	The British Library 96 Euston Road London NW1 2DB Tel: 020 7412 7000 E-mail: npo@bl.uk Web site: http://www.bl.uk/services/preservation/national.html

BIBLIOGRAPHY

National Preservation Office Publications:

NPO Preservation Guidance
Preservation in Practice Series

Preservation of Photographic Material
Author: Susie Clark (1999) National Preservation Office

Good Handling Principles and Practice for Library and Archive Material (2000) National Preservation Office

Photocopying of Library and Archive Material (2000) National Preservation Office

Guidance for exhibiting archive and library materials (2000) National Preservation Office

Preservation Guidelines. National Preservation Office

Amsden, Peter C.   *Images for the future*: a guide to the selection and preservation of photographic and electronic images for personal archives (2000)

Baynes-Cope, A.D. *Caring for books and documents* (1989)

Harvey, Ross   *Preservation in libraries*; principles, strategies and practices for librarians (1993)

INDEX

111

COPYRIGHT PERMISSION

Jewish Ancestors?

A Beginner's Guide to Jewish Genealogy in Great Britain
ISBN: 0-9537669-3-4
Series Editor
Rosemary Wenzerul

NEARING 3000 COPIES SOLD

◆An insight into the world of Jewish genealogy◆
◆A must for the beginner to genealogy◆
◆Packed from cover to cover with useful information◆
◆An inspiration to continue research once started◆
Price: £4.50 + 50p p&p (UK) and £6.00/US$10 (overseas)

Jewish Ancestors?

A Guide to Jewish Genealogy in Germany and Austria
ISBN: 0-9537669-1-8
Written by
Thea Skyte and Randol Schoenberg
Series Editor
Rosemary Wenzerul

◆ An insight into researching your Germany or Austrian family roots◆
◆An informative guide to the archives of available records◆
◆Explains how to obtain the records you thought no longer existed◆
Price: £4.50 + 50p p&p (UK) and £6.00/US$10 (overseas)

Jewish Ancestors?

A Guide to Jewish Genealogy in Latvia & Estonia
ISBN: 0-9537669-2-6
Written by
Arlene Beare
Series Editor
Rosemary Wenzerul

◆ Points you in the right direction for researching your
roots in both the UK and in Latvia & Estonia◆
◆An insight into a host of available records◆
◆Useful tips and information for the genealogical traveller to this area◆
Price: £4.50 + 50p p&p (UK) and £6.00/US$10 (overseas)

Genealogical Resources within the Jewish Home and Family

ISBN: 1 86006 148 6

Written by
Rosemary Wenzerul

◆ Ideal gift for all the family◆
◆Will help document your family history for future generations◆
◆Draws attention to the information contained in the documents◆
◆Numerous illustrations◆

Price: £5.95 + 80p p/p (UK) + £2.00 p/p (overseas)

Order form and additional information about the above publications may be seen on the Society's web site: www.jgsgb.org.uk

Available by post from:
Publications Department
The Jewish Genealogical Society of Great Britain
PO Box 180, St. Albans, Herts. AL2 3WH.
(E-mail: publications@jgsgb.org.uk)

Cheques with orders please made payable to:
The Jewish Genealogical Society of Great Britain

Payment by Credit Card: We can accept Visa, Mastercard or Eurocard (please circle type)
PLEASE PRINT CLEARLY

Card No:

Expiry Date: _____/_____   Card Holder: _____

Name of Publication: _____

Quantity: _____   Amount: £_____p_____

Address:

_____

_____

Postcode: _____   Tel No: _____

Signature: _____
PRINT NAME UNDER LINE:

MEMBERSHIP APPLICATION FORM

The Jewish Genealogical Society is a charity run by volunteers, aiming to promote and encourage the study of and research into Jewish genealogy.

MEMBERSHIP APPLICATION

Surname

Forename

Address

Postcode

Tel

Fax

Email

SUBSCRIPTIONS

1 January to 31 December		(please tick)
UK Individual or institution	£32.00	☐
UK Family *	£38.46	☐
Overseas (all)	£30.00	☐

Those who have signed the Gift Aid Declaration overleaf may deduct tax and pay:

Individuals	£25.00	☐
Family	£30.00	☐

Special rates for full time students, registered unemployed and those on similar benefits are available on application.

*Family subscriptions are for two people sharing one copy of our journal Shemot and the JGSGB Newsletter.

50% of the above rates apply if joining after 30 June.

The Jewish Genealogical Society of Great Britain

Registered charity no. 1022738

GIFT AID DECLARATION

I would like the Jewish Genealogical Society of Great Britain to treat all donations I have made since 5 April 2000, and any I make subsequently, as Gift Aid donations.

Signature   Date

Please note: You will need to have paid an amount of income tax or capital gains tax at least equal to the amount of tax we claim back. Please inform us if your personal details change or if you stop paying tax in the UK.
I do not pay UK income tax or capital gains tax. ☐

PAYMENT DETAILS

Subscription	£
Donation	£
TOTAL	£

I enclose my cheque (made payable to JGSGB)

OR I would like to pay by Credit Card (please tick)

Visa ☐   Mastercard ☐   Eurocard ☐

Card No   –   –   –

Expiry Date

Card Holder

Signature

To comply with the Data Protection Act members need to be aware that we are storing personal information electronically and we need their permission to do so.
I give permission for information for the data that I provide on this form to be store and processed by computer (or manually) for the administrative purposes of the Jewish Genealogical Society of Great Britain only.

Signature   Date

Please return this form with your remittance to:
The Membership Secretary
The Jewish Genealogical Society of Great Britain
PO Box 2508
Maidenhead, SL6 8WS

Fax: +44 (0)1628-632059

www.jgsgb.org.uk   Registered charity no. 1022738

Subscription rate may not apply after December 2004